Raising Adults

GETTING KIDS READY FOR THE REAL WORLD

JIM HANCOCK

PIÑON PRESS

P.O. Box 35007, Colorado Springs, Colorado 80935

OUR GUARANTEE TO YOU

We believe so strongly in the message of our books that we are
making this quality guarantee to you. If for any reason you are
disappointed with the content of this book, return the title page
to us with your name and address and we will refund to you the
list price of the book. To help us serve you better, please briefly
describe why you were disappointed. Mail your refund request
to: PiñonPress, P.O. Box 35002, Colorado Springs, CO 80935.

Cover Design by Ray Moore
Photo by Claire Hayden/Tony Stone Images
Creative Team: Ray Moore, Tim Howard, Brad Lewis, Terry Behimer

Some of the anecdotal illustrations in this book are true to life and are
included with the permission of the persons involved. All other illustrations are composites of real situations, and any resemblance to
people living or dead is coincidental.

CIP Data Applied For

For additional copies of this book or the *Raising Adults Learning
Guide*, please call (800) 366-7788.

Printed in the United States of America

1 2 3 4 5 6 7 8 9 10/05 04 03 02 01 00 99

Contents

Read Me

0.0

We hate to see kids

get off on the wrong

foot. They are, after

all, our children,

one way or another.

The premise of this book, *Raising Adults,* is a simple word play. North Americans spend eighteen to twenty-four years raising children. The problem is, when we're done, that's often what we end up with: children. Sure, they're adults, but childish adults who are painfully underprepared for the real world.

Most of us nurturers, when we're not feeling angry or afraid about this result, end up unhappy because things didn't work out the way we hoped. After all, we've come to believe the real world requires skilled, mature adults. And, God help us, we look around to find that's not who we've raised.

All this is, of course, a cliché no more accurate than "the Me Decade" a generation ago. Remember the Me Decade? It started as an entertaining, insightful essay on postwar America. After a few months in the popular press, the Me Decade became *the Me Generation,* meaning Baby Boomers. They said we were self-centered and unreliable. They said we were sex-obsessed, drug-addled, and undisciplined. All we cared about, they said, was feeling good. Which made our mothers blink back tears and our fathers shake their heads gravely, wondering where they went wrong.

They were partly right about us Boomers. And partly wrong. America was, and is, a cultural soup. We stew on a back burner, every generation adding unique flavors to the blend. Generalizations seldom reflect anyone's reality. Some of us went to Vietnam, some to Canada. Most stayed put. Some of us smoked dope, a few of us were Jesus freaks, a lot of us went to college, many of us went to work. We did not end Western civilization. We blended into the soup, bringing our flavors with us.

The generations that followed us are doing more or less the same. Most of our children are, or soon will be, competent, capable, productive, fun human beings. Kids have a way of doing that. They turn adult on us, whether we raise them that way or not.

Still, if we're paying attention, we can't help noticing that some of our offspring couldn't care less about life in the real world. "Real to whom?" they wonder. They are Douglas Coupland's "Generation X." People who don't fit in because they *won't* fit in.

> Demon seed is what they are. Inconsiderate. Spoiled brats.

That was Frank. Sometimes Frank says what I'm thinking. Mostly he mumbles and grumbles. Frank's comments appear here and there throughout *Raising Adults*. Take them for what they're worth.

> If we lost our ideals in *The Big Chill,* well our kids are sorry for us but, frankly, it has nothing to do with them. They don't hate us; they don't hold us in contempt. But they don't admire us either, or feel obliged to listen to us. Still, they're watching. For what, we're not sure. They play by a different set of rules and they won't tell us what they are. Non-rules most likely. Meant to make us crazy so they can cash in on all the loot we're about to inherit from their grandparents—our parents. Well you can keep your un-game to yourselves you wicked brood of . . . Oh. Did I say that out loud? Sorry.

In any event, most kids seem to be doing fine. They're not in jail, nor do they seem likely to go there. They get to school or work most days. They don't carry concealed weapons, traffic in drugs, or consort with prostitutes. They seem to be turning out okay. Perhaps it's benign neglect: We managed to not screw them up. Or maybe it was Providence. Providence was very popular with the founding fathers and mothers. It's in all the early writings; I see no reason we can't invoke it now. And maybe we didn't do such a bad job. Maybe the kids are all right.

Except that some—some days it seems like most—*aren't* doing so well. Generations X and Y and whatever's next are clichés. But those clichés are based on something observable. That observable something is a disturbing level of aimlessness, sadness, anger, fear, violence, and hopelessness. Many of our children reach adulthood with a serious deficit of life skills. They enter their adult years emotionally impotent, unable to cope with pressure, socially unskilled, scholastically underprepared, spiritually undernourished.

I wish I could say these problems belong to someone else. I wish I could say they are urban issues. I'd like to point to out-of-touch rural communities and say, *Look, these folk aren't raising adults.* I wish these were the challenges of single mothers, people of color, the poor. It would give me great satisfaction to say these difficulties afflict only the rich. I wish. But it's not true. We're all in the same boat, me and everyone on my wish list.

The problems long associated with our economic underclass are epidemic in the suburbs too. As early as 1981, someone called it "affluenza," the same behaviors and attitudes slightly upscaled.

> With affluenza, just substitute cocaine for crack. Jägermeister instead of Colt 45. It's breaking and entering instead of knocking off convenience stores. Abortion instead of premature birthing. God, I miss the good old days, when we didn't know about this stuff.

And so we're sad. We hate to see kids get off on the wrong foot. They are, after all, our children, one way or another.

The question is, *What are we going to do about it?*

More than twenty million adolescents call North America home. Including their parents, teenagers have the (admittedly divided) attention of thirty-six million adults. To their parents, add a million middle school and high school teachers, instructors, and coaches. Add half a million church-based youth workers, three million employers, and sixteen million retailers, marketers, officers of the court, and, of course, demographers.[1]

As long as we're counting, let's add that only a fraction of global teens live in North America. Before long, two billion teenagers will inhabit this planet. Let me repeat that so you don't have to reread the sentence: In the years just ahead two *billion* teenagers will call this world their home.

[1]George Barna, *Generation Next* (Ventura, CA: Regal Books, 1995), p. 10.

Is it just me or is that an awful lot of kids hanging out at the mall? Or fighting wars . . . Or spreading disease . . . Or building and buying things . . . Or solving planetary problems . . .

[2]*Time*, June 9, 1997, p. 58. As of 2000, they're twenty-four to thirty-five years old. [3]*Business Week*, February 15, 1999, p. 82. Frankly, these numbers are a jumble. The *Time* number includes births between 1965 and 1977. The *Business Week* number includes births between 1979 and 1994. I don't want to alarm anyone, but we're missing someone. [4] I'm no happier with demographic definitions of Generations X and Y than I was with merely statistical descriptions of the Me Generation. Did you ever hear of a book called *How to Lie with Statistics*? This is an example of that. To see what Douglas Coupland, who popularized the term Generation X, meant, go to page 33.

More counting: Depending on whose numbers you like, there are somewhere around forty-five million Generation X Americans.[2] They are followed by about sixty million younger siblings—the ones some people refer to as Generation Y, for reasons that escape me.[3] These are the real kids of today, aged six to twenty-three years as of 2000. Of course, all these numbers assume you're willing to accept a purely demographic definition of Generation X, which I'm not.[4]

Included in these figures is an emerging population of young adults who live a sort of extended adolescence—young men and women who are, in many ways, more like old boys and girls. They remain semidependent on their parents or on public welfare systems. They may or may not be students, may or may not work. They don't pay significant taxes because they don't have significant incomes—at least on the table.

Men in this extended boyhood are inordinately responsible for teenage pregnancies. They're legally adult but functionally adolescent males making babies with underage women. The time-honored American custom of senior boys dating freshman girls now extends into the decade of those boys' twenties. The girls are still likely to be fifteen. One American president called it child abuse. Who can argue with that?

What we can argue is that those men—many of them—are products of parenting in a larger system that raises *children*.

That's no excuse. But it may help us interpret otherwise baffling behavior. At the risk of being obvious, how surprised should we be when someone raised without a sense of responsibility, without an appreciation for cause and effect, acts irresponsibly and causes regrettable effects?

Enough already! What are we supposed to do about it, you and me? We feel sad and guilty for raising children when the assignment was to raise adults. More than sad. We're embarrassed by the looks we're pretty sure we get from our parents; we're afraid of the consequences of our cultural (and perhaps personal) failures; we're trying—hoping—to do better.

Fair enough. It's a start.

⁓⁓

This book is about beginning—from right where we are—to raise adults. It's about how we added our flavors to the cultural soup and how our children flavor it now. It's about practical things we can do to be better moms and dads, better teachers, coaches, youth workers, mentors, employers, and law enforcement officers.

This book is not about assigning blame and beating each other up.

I happen to believe we got here more or less by accident. This is not a theological declaration; I just don't think anybody set out to screw up.

FOR MORE ON ADOLESCENT PREGNANCY, GO TO PAGE **84.**

I don't think my parents or grandparents were particularly bad people. Broken, sure. But not bad.

> **Have we ever gotten a good model of parenting in history? —Eli**

That was Eli. He's one of a handful of friends whose comments appear here and there in *Raising Adults*. Eli is a twenty-year-old college junior from Oregon. Alice grew up in southern California. She's twenty-three and just starting graduate school. Ben is fourteen years old and goes to middle school in Colorado. Brian is a twenty-year-old college student living in Washington state. Kate is my daughter(!). She's twenty-two, working for a year in Alabama at her first post-college job. I've known most of these guys since they were young adolescents. Now that they're adults (except Ben, who's right in the middle of adolescence), I think they give a good perspective on how our culture is doing at *Raising Adults*.

Eli makes a good point. Some people idealize the parenting of the past. But traditional parenting, or whatever you want to call it, was another part of the cultural stew—both the good and the bad.

My mother grew up in a family of displaced farm people. My grandfather left his job as a traveling salesman to work the land my grandmother inherited when she was widowed. They lost the farm. Then, when they moved to Depression-era Jacksonville, Florida, they simply lost their way. I know my grandfather worked hard but he never found a way back to where he knew which way was up. They never fully recovered, financially or otherwise. My grandmother was frustrated to

death by the whole thing. Literally. She died too young. Afraid, angry, disappointed, she lost heart.

My father's parents died before he was two years old and his older sisters and brothers raised him. They did the best they could.

Tell me. In what perfect world of yesterday did my parents learn parenting? Why would my father know the first thing about being a good dad? At whose knee could my mother have learned the nurturing arts?

A psychologist might have predicted the adults my parents would become.

My dad was out of control. An attractive, intelligent, undisciplined, spendthrift, compulsive dreamer. He shot himself in the foot over and over until he didn't have a leg to stand on. He neglected his children for the sake of his work. He neglected his wife for adventures with women he barely knew.

My mom grew up to live the life of a lovely, personable, competent, hard-working, frightened realist. At a time when most women in her social set stayed at home, my mom worked to make the mortgage and car payments. She wanted more time with her children, but she was busy ensuring our physical well-being. I don't have a clue what kind of income my parents had, but I'm pretty sure my father spent everything both of them made—and then some.

After a shocking divorce (no one knew anything was wrong), my father and mother remarried others. Some people marry the same type of person again and again. Not my parents. The second time around, they married people who couldn't have been more different.

When I was nineteen, my mother married an older man and built a lasting, respectful marriage. My father had already remarried because he had to. The young woman was pregnant.

My parents were ordinary folk: broken, needy, imperfect, human. Could they have tried harder? I have no idea. They gave it their best shot. My sister turned out well. The jury is still out in my case.

I can't find the bad guys in my family. The inept, unskilled, foolish, shattered guys, yes. In abundance. That's what I am. I suspect it's what you are too (though you'll have to vote on that yourself). Eugene O'Neill wrote, "Man is born broken. He lives by mending. The grace of God is glue."[5] That's the starting point for *Raising Adults*. From that baseline, we'll try to generate new perceptions and aptitudes, develop new skills, mend the brokenness. *Raising Adults* is about building and rebuilding relationships that nourish and nurture people to adulthood. It's for parents, teachers, mentors, and youth workers who want to be proactive. This is a book about hope and help to do a good job starting from where we are right now—not where we're supposed to be.

[5] quoted in Anne Lamott's *Traveling Mercies* (New York: Pantheon, 1999), p. 112.

> How about us who are geared to someday become parents? *Basically,* will this book convince *me* to want to raise children/adults? —Eli

*Raising Adult*s is for people determined to be more intentional, more skillful, more realistic, more effective. It's for those who wish they could retrofit their relationships with deeper understanding and love.

They can. You can. I'm doing it, and I'm no prize. You may find me a bit cynical, a bit crass, a bit irreverent. I'm all those things; plus I'm working my way through more than a little anger, more than a little fear, and a whole lot of failure. I'm grateful to the women in my life: Susan, my partner in marriage since 1972, and Kate, our daughter since 1976. They love me as if I were as good as the image I've tried to maintain outside our household. They're helping me become that person. Meanwhile, I'm just a reasonably intelligent man figuring out that—as it seems the universe doesn't revolve around me—maybe I can learn something about doing my job in the universe. In the meantime, I'm afraid I'm a Baby Boomer clear to the bone. A lot of what you've heard about Boomers, you'll find in me. Sorry. So, as you read on, know that when I say "we," I usually mean Boomer parents who grew up swimming in the same soup.

One last bit of housekeeping. It may feel like you're reading three books instead of one—which is actually a good deal, assuming you paid for only one.

- Sections 1.0 through 1.4 examine why we're the way we are. It's a taste of the cultural soup we grew up in. Part One answers the question: *Why is it so hard to raise adults these days?*
- Sections 2.0 through 2.6 explore solid relational skills that will make us better parents (teachers, youth workers, coaches), starting right where we are. Part Two answers the question: *What does it take to raise 21st century adults?*

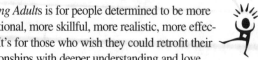

•Sections 3.0-4.0 look at the soup our kids are in and offer concrete strategies for meeting them right where they are. Part Three answers the question: *How do we get what it takes to raise adults?*

You may be tempted to jump right into Part Two or Part Three. Fair enough. It's your book and I won't try to stop you. But, for what it's worth, Part One lays a useful foundation for understanding and applying what comes after.

And one more thought: I want to tell you why this book is important to me. I want you to know my hope for you as you read:

For a long time, when hurting, at-risk kids and parents came to me for help, I wanted to know—the "judge" in me wanted to know—*Did she jump or was she pushed?* Things like that matter to the judge. But after awhile, broken and battered myself, compassion posed a new question: *Does it matter? She's broken. What now?*

That's my hope for you now: that you'll be able to look at things as they are and ask, *What now?*

TO KNOW MORE ABOUT ME, GO TO PAGES **44** [GUARANTEE] AND **176** [ONE BOAT].

Dear Mom and Dad

1.0

Our parents

did something

completely

different.

The Great Depression and World War II (the war after the war to end all wars) tumbled one on top of the other and landed on our moms and dads. (I'm generally referring to the generation born in the 1920s and 30s.) It was a catastrophic double whammy. But as the smoke cleared, America strode out of the rubble like John Wayne. Victorious. But not *just* victorious. America emerged from that war with a supercharged, take-no-prisoners economy that electrified the world.

> We won! *Our* way of life; not theirs! There was no place we wouldn't go, nothing we couldn't do. We had big plans! *Really big!* America! Marching together into *the future!*
>
> That's what it was all about: Manifest Destiny in full flower; the American Century. (Music swells, fireworks light the Stars and Stripes against a jet black sky.)

The American Future was dreamed up by the brightest, shiniest Planners of Tomorrow, Grand Marshals in the Parade of Progress, men who saw the way we were and imagined the way we could be. They couldn't have been clearer about the next step and it was all about *cities*. They knew in their bones that millions of young Americans whose parents moved to the cities for jobs in the thirties, and millions more who came to join the war effort in the forties, had come to stay. These young people marched in six-eight time to the beat of the city. Speed! Access! Diversity! Mobility! Information! Stuff! They would never be satisfied with the pace of America's small towns and farms. "We'll see you for Thanksgiving, Granny; but we'll be *living* in the City!"

That's why nearly everyone was surprised by what happened next.

Our parents thought all this was interesting but not fascinating. They didn't make a big deal about it—they simply declined to join the parade.

The social architects were partly right. Most of our parents didn't return to small-town America. But they didn't exactly stay in the cities either. All those young men came back from WWII to marry all those young women sardined into America's factory and government towns. It was too close for comfort. A housing shortage blew city rents right through the roof. These young Americans weren't seeking rural bliss, but they weren't ready to be packed together like sailors on a ship either. Something had to give.

Our parents did something completely different. They took their VA loans and invented something brand new (drumroll, please): the suburbs.

A BRIEF HISTORY OF THE BURBS—In 1946, Levitt and Sons constructed the first phase of a planned community of inexpensive, mass-produced homes in Nassau County, on Long Island, outside New York City, and the American suburb was born. The master plan included everything a young family could want: schools, shopping, and recreation right in the neighborhood. That first suburban community was called Levittown, New York. By 1951 Levittown was a done deal and Levitt and Sons moved on to Bucks County, Pennsylvania, where they built—you guessed it—Levittown, PA. At the end of the fifties, Levitt and Sons redeveloped a three-hundred-year old township in New Jersey, changing its name to—that's right—Levittown. Four years later the township reclaimed its ancestral name, Willingboro—but folks passing through couldn't help noticing it looked a lot like Levittown.

And that's where, for better and worse, most of us grew up: near cities and towns, in housing developments that didn't exist before the war.

Over the next several years, our grandparents shouldered a massive tax burden as many of our fathers converted GI Bill dollars to college degrees before joining their dads in business. About six million of our mothers and aunts continued working as they had during the war.[1] The payoff, in disposable dollars for everyone, climbed right off the charts.

Wartime technology was a postwar gold mine. Nylon and a zillion other textiles; paper-thin aluminum and a bizillion more lightweight building materials; radar and a gazillion electronic technologies—all these became big business in their own right. The defense industry didn't wind down after the war—a first in modern history—and American men and women continued cranking out engines of war with "never again" zeal.

C. Wright Mills claimed this was a new military industrial complex at the beck and call of a new kind of ruling class who held power because they ran business and government, not because they owned property. Mills said the military industrial complex would be a bad thing for America and the world.[2] His untimely death in 1962 generated a conspiracy theory of X-Files proportions.

So there they were: young Americans; going to college, making babies, living in the suburbs, working in the cities, building a new life. But not the new life the social architects predicted. Not a life anybody ever lived before—in America or anywhere else.

They parked fishing boats and travel trailers in the driveways of their suburban homes. They worked like mad all year, then took vacations on superhighways, crisscrossing the nation from coast to coast.

As much as they enjoyed traditional spots like Miami and Niagara Falls, these mobile Americans built the fortunes of places nobody heard of before

The most ambitious highway of them all, the twelve-year, $25-billion Interstate Highway project okayed by Congress in 1944 and funded in 1956, actually took thirty-five years and $50 billion to complete.

the war. Walt and Roy Disney grew Disneyland from an orange grove; Bugsy Siegel and Meyer Lansky raised Las Vegas like a Phoenix from the desert. And young Americans made them rich.

And did I mention our parents had babies? Boy did they have babies.

[1] David Halberstam, *The Fifties* (New York: Fawcett Books, 1993).

[2] C. Wright Mills, *The Power Elite*, (London: Oxford University Press, 1956).

You woulda thought they were returning to the farm. You'da thought they needed to raise enough farm hands to run the family operation with a plow and no mules. You'da thought we were a nation of rabbits! Fertility! Soldiers and sailors came home from Europe and North Africa and Asia and bam! Their wives delivered babies nine months and twenty minutes later!

Our moms and dads were a fertile lot. The population increase from 1940 to 1950 was more than double the increase from 1930 to 1940.

There are stories of young men comparing military campaign notes in maternity waiting rooms.

"Lessee, it's June '46; the bomb dropped last August . . . So, you were in the Pacific when the Emperor surrendered. Am I right?"

"Mmm . . . Good guess. Actually I came back from Berlin, walking the frontier with the Soviets."

"What? I thought you said you were a Marine!"

"Who said anything about Marines! Airborne, my friend. All the way."

Our parents were, quite simply, a different breed. Raised in the biggest economic bust in America's history, they fueled one of the biggest booms. They came of age winning America's last "good" war, but the horror of the victory was emotionally debilitating.

Many of our mothers watched helplessly as lots of our fathers shut down. Permanently. Many of us grew up with male role models a lot more like the Marlboro Man than, say, Santa Claus. They were silent, stoic, distant, disconnected from their spouses and children—everything but work, really. Sure it's a stereotype, but nobody made it up. Our fathers had other, secret lives. Some because they went overseas, others because they didn't.

And what do you suppose was the effect on the 110,000 Americans of Japanese descent who lost everything when they were relocated to camps from the California mountains to the Mississippi River? Hard to say. They didn't talk about it much.

James Jones wrote about his war with horrible realism in *The Thin Red Line*. Joseph Heller wrote about his with equally horrible comedy in *Catch 22*. Everyone else went by the numbers. How many went ashore, how many fell from the sky, how much ground was covered, how many lives were lost.

Or they remained silent.

Maybe our fathers talked to each other— I don't know. Maybe they talked about this stuff down at the lodge, or with their hunting buddies, their drinking pals, their shrinks, their mistresses. But not with us. They couldn't say it, or we couldn't hear it.

Our fathers kept an awful lot to themselves. What they couldn't keep quiet was their growing obsession with having done the right thing. That aching desperation echoes in the closing moments of Steven Spielberg's *Saving Private Ryan*. It's fifty years since D-Day and Ryan pleads, "Am I a good man? Tell me I lived a good life."

World War II Casualties

The Good Guys
Belgium: 88,000 dead; 76,000 civilians. Brazil: 1,000 dead. Australia: 24,000 dead. Canada: 38,000 dead. India: 24,000 dead. New Zealand: 10,000 dead. South Africa: 7,000 dead. The United Kingdom: 357,000 dead; 92,673 civilians. The British Colonies: 7,000 dead. China: 1,310,224 killed, wounded, or in prison. Czechoslovakia: 225,000 dead; 215,000 civilians. Denmark: 4,000 dead; half of them civilians. France: 563,000 dead; 350,000 civilians. Greece: 413,000 dead; 325,000 civilians. Netherlands: 208,000 dead; 200,000 civilians. Norway: 10,000 dead; 7,000 civilians. Poland (better sit down): 5.8 million dead, of whom 5,675,000 were civilians. Philippines: 118,000 dead; 91,000 civilians. United States: 298,000 dead; 6,000 civilians. USSR: (still sitting, I hope) 18 million dead; 7,000,000 civilians. Yugoslavia: 1,505,000 dead; 1,200,000 civilians.

The Bad Guys
Bulgaria: 20,000 dead; half civilians. Finland: 84,000 dead; 2,000 civilians. Germany: 4.2 million dead; 780,000 civilians. Hungary: 490,000 dead; 290,000 civilians. Italy: 395,000 dead; 152,941 civilians. Japan: 1.972 million dead; 672,000 civilians (most on August 6 and 9, 1945). Romania: 500,000 dead; 200,000 civilians.[3]

I wept when I heard it; you can't make that stuff up.

The picture is not less complicated for our mothers.

On September 2, 1945, the rules changed. Japan surrendered unconditionally, ending one war and beginning another. The new war was about identity—who would they all be in the new world order? Many of our mothers would be numbered among the casualties.

Role models? Don't know any.—Brian

I can think of five women who are my role models—they're all very different, but have one thing in common: They are genuine, real, honest, vulnerable.—Alice

Our female role models were, as a class, deeply conflicted. Imagine leaving home to join the war effort, taking a serious job, doing serious work in a serious cause. Forget *Can-Do!* spirit. Franklin Roosevelt rose from his wheelchair and said this was *Do or Die!* And nearly everyone believed it.

By golly, America's women rose to the challenge. Women built tanks and airplanes and battleships. Women manufactured bullets and bombs. But not all. Some stayed home and worked the farms and stores. They kept paying taxes, kept rationing gasoline and sugar, kept raising sons and sending them to Europe or North Africa or the Pacific, kept raising daughters and sending them to Detroit or Pittsburgh or Oakland or Washington, D.C.

[3] Encyclopædia Britannica CD 98, World War II Casualties.

[4] David Halberstam, *The Fifties* (New York: Fawcett Books, 1993).

Imagine . . . take a moment . . . Imagine the post-partum-sized depression when those services were no longer required. *If not my services, then what? Am I no longer required? Who, exactly, am I now?*

It's not the first time American women stepped into the gap. Female colonists and pioneers did the hard work of colonizing and pioneering until they died. Their daughters or granddaughters settled down eventually. Not the first generation though. They cleared fields, crossed rivers, drove teams, and mended canvas. They did their part. And no question about it, so did our mothers—eight million of them during the war.

But this time there was an expiration date. *May 8, 1945: VE Day; well done! Now we shift everything to the Pacific Theater. August 6: The atom bomb bursts over Hiroshima. The end is near. September 2: Stand down. A grateful nation thanks you. Now, go home.*

And, just like that, American women were out of a job. The good news and the bad news were the same news.

In the 1930s, more than half the states had laws against hiring married women, but all that changed when we needed them in the forties. Then at the end of the war, some eight hundred thousand women were laid off in the aircraft industry within two months of the peace. The combined layoffs of women totaled two million by 1948.[4]

I don't know if women spoke much more about *their* experiences than men did. Perhaps it would have seemed un-American, maybe unwomanly, to complain.

Wait, there's more. Now imagine watching the one you love shut down. Imagine having babies in a flurry, moving to the suburbs, taking on a clerical job to help with the mortgage—spread thin between the workplace and *your place* as a wife and mother, as a homemaker. Meanwhile, the guy across the living room, the one who shares your bed, gradually checks out into work or booze or both. You hardly know him any more. And the children never knew the man you fell in love with. What now?

As the forties ended, our parents were sucked into a vortex of change that made their heads spin. Geographical and social displacement, a gender crisis almost nobody talked about, babies *everywhere*, exploding college enrollment, a religious revival on the West Coast, labor-management disputes in the cities, globalization and an enlarged tax burden driven by the Marshall Plan's massive foreign aid, high-tech innovation, economic growth, and work, work, *work!* Good Golly, Miss Molly, those people could work!

They threw themselves into the race, redirecting the horses of war onto an economic fast-track unmatched on earth. And they relished the fruit of their labors, forsaking their waste-not-want-not past with giddy pleasure. *Their* parents gathered 'round the radio, heard promises of a chicken in every pot, and hoped for a better day. Our parents worked overtime to put two cars in the driveway, four pots on the electric range, and a television in the living room.

Did our grandparents watch all this and wonder who raised these people? Their coming of age was no less dramatic. They were buoyed along on an economic and technological high tide at the turn of the last century, only to be shipwrecked by the Great War in Europe and the 1917 flu epidemic that killed maybe 30 million people worldwide. The survivors of that generation were called the Lost Generation. Not exactly a hula hoop experience.

Television—wonder of wonders! It was the Saturday matinee—minus Milk Duds but with all the comforts of home. Even in the beginning, when the square screens displayed test patterns most of the day, our parents had access to sights and sounds most human beings never expected to see in their own homes. Buffalo Bob and Howdy Doody for the kids. Live comedy on *Your Show of Shows*. Broadway and Hollywood actors on *Playhouse 90*. And, perhaps most wondrous of all, *the news*.

Our parents were the first generation of human beings to get their news on television, complete with pictures. Who would've thought it! To catch fifteen minutes of *today's* news with Douglas Edwards? Unprecedented! To watch the coronation of Queen Elizabeth and sneak out to the kitchen for a glass of iced tea? Mind-boggling! To follow Edward R. Murrow right into the homes and offices of celebrities and politicians for real-time, unedited question-and-answer sessions; to watch him ask Paul Newman and Joanne Woodward, Richard Nixon, and Joe McCarthy the questions every American wanted to ask.

And this was no glossed-over Movie Tone newsreel! Viewers knew Murrow would hold people's feet to the fire until they answered or flat-out refused him. Nothing like it, ever, in the history of the world!

Our parents were there when it happened. We happened to be there too, born into the moment. But *they were there* when everything changed.

Television was the great equalizer. Television was the fire circle—the place where the tribe gathered to hear stories about the world. Anyone could know anything, regardless of race, creed, color, gender, education, geography, or age. *Anyone could know anything!* This was why they fought the war and they didn't even know it. This was the world made safe for democracy—freedom of information right now, without leaving home.

And the pictures didn't lie. Paul and Joanne were fabulously happy—anyone could see it. Joseph McCarthy was hard and ambitious—who could miss it? And Richard Nixon looked, frankly, shifty.

Much has been made of the fact that Baby Boomers were the first generation to grow up with television. But that doesn't mean television's impact is unique to us. In fact, to us, television is a *transparent technology*. We turn it on and it works, much as it has since we were little. We hardly ever *thought* about television; it was a given. Oh, the NBC Peacock in living color was a nice upgrade. And remote control. And cable. But these are extensions to television, improvements on the design. Our parents had the amazing experience of seeing it for the first time.

Technology is like that: wonderful for quite a while before it becomes ordinary, then transparent. Electric lights and telephones have been transparent for a century. Light switches changed my grandfather's life by extending his productive hours into the night. Telephones changed my grandmother's life, extending her ability to talk with relatives a hundred miles away. By the time my parents came along, electric lights and telephones were no big deal; they just were. But television!

> *When television first came in the early 1950s, Japan's leading electronics executive said, ". . . the Japanese simply do not have the money to buy television sets." Two years later television penetration in Japan was almost as high as it was in the U.S. . . . They simply moved more and more of their disposable income to TV because it gave them access to a world from which they had been isolated for centuries. It was not a product but a whole new way of life.*
>
> **—Peter Drucker in Forbes *magazine,***
> ***October 5, 1998, page 170***

Among other things, TV raised the bar for keeping up with the Joneses. With a flicker of phosphorescent light, the Joneses weren't just next door. They were also in Omaha and San Francisco. Or maybe it's more useful to say the Joneses of Omaha and San Francisco were suddenly as close as the ones next door.

That's a big deal: seeing all those Joneses— how they lived, what they drove and wore, hearing what they thought and how they voted. In a snap,

our parents entered a national conversation on everything from dish soap to cold war politics with equal intensity. Actually, that may not be true. The dish soap discussion was considerably more shrill.

We hold these things to be self-evident. We take them for granted and always have, because for us they've always been there. Getting our attention these days is not easy. We've seen and heard so much. For our parents, television was the biggest thing anybody ever saw—a Space-Age miracle, a window on the world, a time machine. Television changed everything.

Meanwhile, the kids were getting into trouble and nobody even noticed.

What did your daddy do in the war? How about your mom?

How much do you really know about your parents' young adulthood? How do you feel about that?

What are your earliest recollections of the neighborhood where you grew up?

What's your earliest recollection of television?

The First Wave

1.1

For the first time . . .

classroom focus

shifted from what

students learned to

what teachers taught.

History books hardly mention it, but, in 1951, six years after the war ended, the day after Labor Day, give or take, a tide swept over America.

That was the day the first wave of Baby Boomers broke on America's schools. Kindergarten classes, which averaged about fifteen students in 1950, had more than thirty in 1951. The first day of school was chaos in many places. Imagine thousands of five-year-olds standing against the walls of small classrooms at eight o'clock in the morning—their first morning of school ever. There are too few chairs, too few pencils, too few teachers. Maybe you don't have to imagine. Maybe you were one of them.

The biggest surprise is, *no one saw them coming!* They were five years old for crying out loud! They were ready for kindergarten; kindergarten wasn't ready for them.

It was a moment of crisis in education. It became a quandary in child rearing because the response to this flood of students seems to have been:

Make More Desks,
Build Larger Classrooms

Just like that, from sea to shining sea, too many students and too few teachers became the norm.

You already know what happened, but here it is again for the record. For the first time, in a nation committed to universal education, classroom focus shifted from what students learned to what teachers taught.

- Teachers, who previously gave personal attention to each student throughout the day, now spent a large part of their energy on crowd control.
- Students, whose older siblings had time to engage their teachers and fellow students in meaningful discussion, became note-takers. The most successful pupils learned to discern which points in the teachers' lectures were important.

Today I am announcing a nationwide search for the individual who first voiced the immortal question: "Will this be on the test?" He or she will be enshrined. Or maybe pilloried.

- Monolog replaced dialog overnight. The school day, which, a year before included personal attention for every student, now consisted of as much lecture as the children could stand, followed by work sheets, list-making, and rote memorizing, followed by more lecture.
- Writing was gradually replaced by multiple-choice testing—my Earth Science teacher called it multiple *guess*. Multiple-choice tests could be administered smoothly and graded quickly. Eventually, the tests were standardized nationwide.
- Classroom discussion, such as it was, tended to be dominated by a few students at the front of the room. The unskilled, the uncertain, and the shy hid out in the back or, worse, were hidden by the bodies in front of them.

Fast forward a dozen years. It is 1963. The Civil Rights movement is in full swing. The Supreme Court rules on school-sponsored prayer. We are unaware that President Kennedy is nearing the end of his rope even as he launches the United States into the space race and threatens to heat up the Cold War. Schoolchildren practice duck-and-cover routines while construction companies do big business on fallout shelters. And, in the Fall, for the first time anyone can remember, school achievement declines. The Class of '64 doesn't do as well as the classes before them. In suicide, pregnancy, and crime rates, they do worse.

A year passes. Kennedy is dead. The Civil Rights Act is law. The British mount a prime-time invasion of North America (pushing west out of Liverpool, the Beatles take New York in a single day). The Class of '65 achieves less than the Class of '64.

A year passes. U.S. military advisors are on the ground in some place called Vietnam. Things get out of hand at the Monterey Pop Festival in California. The Class of '66 achieves less than the Class of '65.

And so it goes, year after year, America's children achieving less than their grandparents in the boom at the turn of the last century, less than their own parents in the depths of the Depression. What gives?

One theory ties the decline in achievement and increased juvenile crime, teenage pregnancy, and suicide to the Supreme Court decision banning *compulsory, school-sponsored* prayer. An interesting notion.

I was in grade school when I saw Madeline Murray O'Hare, the plaintiff in the school prayer case, on a television talk show—seems to me it was the *Tennessee Ernie Ford* program but I'm not certain. I recall something about her son being forced to pray at school. I understood her to be an atheist and I understood that to be a bad thing. Other than the recollection that my parents were upset by the Court's decision, I don't remember much else. I suppose we must have stopped saying the Lord's Prayer at school about then, but I don't remember the day it happened. I recall more than a few God-if-you-help-me-on-this-test-I-promise-I'll-study-for-the-next-one prayers—if you care to call that prayer. I don't recall any overall effect on our multiple guess scores when we stopped reciting what my Catholic friends called "The Our Father." I could be wrong.

Here's another theory: The first wave of Baby Boom school children started their senior year in the fall of 1963. They're the ones who began without enough desks or teachers for a traditional education in Readin', 'Ritin,' and 'Rithmetic. They're the ones whose parents worked day and night to provide what *they* didn't have as children—*stuff*; material possessions. The Class of '64 were the first children who grew up mostly in suburbs instead of small towns and old neighborhoods. They grew up without steady exposure to grandparents, aunts, uncles, and lifelong family friends. They were the ones who, raised with the new medium of television, learned to absorb information a little differently from those who came before. They learned to think differently. Parents of the Class of 1964 didn't know what to do with them—anybody could see it in parental reaction to pompadours, T-shirts and jeans, rock & roll, and "race music." The kids sure felt it. That was obvious from the Saturday night cruising cultures—kids burning cheap gas in fast cars for no reason other than to be *out*, meaning *not home*. They embraced heroes like James Dean, Little Richard, Buddy Holly, and Richie Valens, then Beat writers like Ginsberg and Burroughs. "Edgar Rice Burroughs?" their fathers would ask, "the Tarzan guy?" "No, Dad: William Burroughs, the *Naked Lunch* guy. Gad! You are so square."

More than 53 million children enrolled for school in the Fall of 1999—the greatest number in US history.
—*NBC Nightly News, August 16, 1999*

And yep, these were also the hippie kids who hung out in parks, smoking dope and pitching Frisbees. *And* they were the leading edge of a wave of rising crime, juvenile pregnancy, and suicide. A wave the rest of us followed and follow still. I think it was the Frisbees.

Big Basic Question: Does it make sense to attribute the decline in achievement and the rise in public health problems to things that occurred when the Class of '64 were seniors (namely, the Supreme Court decision on school-sponsored prayer)?

Perhaps most trivial of all these indicators is the decline in scholastic achievement and test scores. Compared to a growing prison population (not to mention the growing number of victims); compared to growing teenage pregnancy rates (not to mention the cost to single mothers and their children and the numbing effect on prodigal fathers of sex for sex's sake); compared to the tragic loss of life—the suicidal abandonment of hope—lower test scores hardly seem worth mentioning. But school achievement is concrete; it seems like something we might be able to do something about. So, of course we would mention it. Of course we would fixate on what to do about those darn schools.

Big Basic Question Answered: I think students in the Class of '64 were shaped by the seventeen years it took them to arrive in their senior year. How could it be otherwise? The Class of '40 grew up in the adversity of the 1930s, graduated, and went off to fight the war. They had no control over the circumstances of their lives—they were children. For better and worse, their Depression-era upbringing shaped them. How could it be otherwise? That was their cultural soup. Five years later, when they conceived the first wave of a new generation, how could those children not be shaped by the fifties?

Come to think of it, How could our kids not be shaped by the soup they're in?

 What are some of your early recollections about school?

Zeitgeist

1.2

He wrote incisively, surgically revealing our cultural innards. I was dazzled, horrified, embarrassed, thrilled, exposed.

Generation Xers are the children of the Me Decade. Remember?

August 23, 1976, about ten weeks before Jimmy Carter would be elected president, the cover of *New York* magazine featured thirty young Americans in T-shirts from the colors-not-found-in-nature collection at Monkey Wards. I believe we can assume the pants were polyester-blend flairs. The women all wore Brady sister do's. The men had helmet-hair, exactly like mine. They were all white, or near enough.

The headline read:

"Tom Wolfe Reports on America's New Great Awakening: The "Me" Decade"

The shirts bore the single word, "ME." Inside the magazine, Tom Wolfe described my generation of Anglo-Americans—postwar Baby Boomers—with stunning accuracy. He wrote incisively, surgically revealing our cultural innards. I was dazzled, horrified, embarrassed, thrilled, exposed.

Wolfe recalled the 1961 Clairol ad in which a woman said, "If I've only one life to live, let me live it as a blond." There, in one line, was the spirit of our age—our cultural zeitgeist: If I have only one life to live, let me live it . . . however I want, wherever I want, doing whatever I want, with whomever I want.

Baby Boomers embraced the idea like we thought it up ourselves. If our parents struck out in nearly the opposite direction from their parents, I suppose we split the difference in search of *our* American dream.

Our parents left their extended families for life in the suburbs; we tried, at least briefly, to reconstruct extended families in communes.

Our parents embraced everything shiny, synthetic, and plastic; we made plastic a dirty word and took up macramé and sand candles.

Our parents calmed their nerves with valium and cocktails; we preferred hemp and beer. They set their neurons firing with prescription pep pills; we cooked up all manner of stimulants, mixing them freely with psychedelics—organic and otherwise.

The only drugs we ever really agreed on were alcohol and nicotine.

Our parents joined our grandparents in a war that took them to the end of the world; we declined an invitation to make the world safe for democracy in southeast Asia.

What was unspeakable for our parents, we spoke right out loud. What they kept hidden, we did in broad daylight. Free speech and free sex; if it can be thought, it can be uttered; if it feels good, do it.

In some ways, our parents' departure from tradition was more polar than ours, but it was certainly more polite. They didn't storm out of town, they just never came all the way back from the war. They took the old joke seriously: They didn't go away mad, they just went away.

When we went away, they knew it. We ranted, we raved, we demonstrated in the streets. We burned draft cards and undergarments and flags and, sadly, bridges. Maybe my perceptions are wrong about this, but I know hardly anyone of my generation who hasn't needed major reconstruction to repair broken relationships with their parents. Your mileage may vary. I hope so.

But even with the noisy exit, we didn't go much farther than the backyard. Our lives are, by and large, less different from those of our next-elders than their lives were from our grandparents' lives. A few of us moved to gentrified city-centers. A few moved to small towns. But, for the most part, we live in the rings of sprawling suburbs beyond our parents' suburbs.

I live half a continent away from the suburb where I grew up, but the neighborhoods aren't significantly different. The houses are bigger now; most have more bathrooms than people (a happy upgrade), but a cultural anthropologist would recognize them as generically the same.

That's nothing like the change my parents experienced from infancy to adulthood. Having *any* indoor bathroom was a big deal. Running water, electric appliances, paved streets . . . all these now-transparent technologies were new to my parents in mid-childhood.

I hate to admit this, but I suppose I've followed my parents' footsteps—in every practical way—more than they followed the lead of the generation before them. Honestly, I don't know why I hate to admit it; I just do.

Which leads me to wonder about my kid's generation. They seem so *other* to most of us—foulmouthed slackers, horny underachievers, inscrutable Xers—these, these, children of the Me Decade. They're not very different from us. Not very different at all.

꧁꧂

1976. Tom Wolfe is right about us—at least in the broad strokes. But what the popular media do with his insights seems all wrong.

"The 'Me' Decade" is on the street August 23. In a matter of weeks the media turn the Me Decade into the *Me Generation*. By that time no one means what Wolfe meant. They aren't describing the spirit of the age—that cultural *zeitgeist* we inherited and embellished from our parents. They mean people born when we were born. They mean *us* and no one else. The Me Generation is defined by demographics and the question on everybody's mind is: "How do we sell them stuff?"

How do you sell to people reputedly driven by self-interest? Nothing, apparently, could be easier. And so the sixties become the eighties. *Our* youth culture, darkly celebrated by Buck Henry and Mike Nichols in *The Graduate* (1967), lasts what seems like just a moment, its death conceded by Lawrence Kasdan in *The Big Chill* (1983).

Baby Boomers took to business in a big way. We spent big dollars building suburbs out beyond the suburbs. We upgraded our parents' shopping centers to megamalls; imported German and Japanese cars from former manufacturers of tanks and bombers; elected Ronald Reagan and George Bush because they would be good for business, . . . Some of us had the nerve to display Grateful Dead stickers in the rear windows of our four-door imports (not the skeletons, just those cute dancing bears—you know who you are).

What happened to us? For some, the answer was, "Nothing! Just shut up! We ended The War. We made Nixon resign. We invented Earth Day. We went to Woodstock: Three days of PeaceLove&Understanding! How can you say we're self-absorbed!"

But that's exactly what they said. Tom Wolfe updated his vision of the Me Decade in his 1987 novel, *Bonfire of the Vanities* (the book, not the awful Brian DePalma film), and again in *A Man in Full* (1998). Wolfe's characters wander, self-consumed and thoroughly disoriented, through these comic horrors. Wolfe's vision goes beyond caricature. God help us, these characters are just like us: our youth spent, our idealism gone to seed. How could this happen!

No one seems to know; it just did. We laid aside our macramé, got real jobs, and spent money like there was no tomorrow.

And we made babies too—not as fast as our parents, but in large numbers—all the while divorcing each other at unparalleled rates. In 1970, there were about 2,159,000 marriages and about 708,000 divorces—one divorce for every three marriages. The median duration of the marriages that ended was not quite seven years. After that, things got a little weird.

From 1975 to 1995 there was roughly one divorce for every two marriages: about 35,696,000 marriages and about 17,543,000 divorces. Through 1990, the median duration of the marriages that ended hovered between six and a half and just over seven years. The number of children involved in divorce remained constant

[1] U.S. Census Bureau, Vital Statistics Report, as of October, 1998 and U.S. Census Bureau, Census Brief, CENBR/97-1, September 1997.
[2] U.S. Census Bureau, Census Brief, CENBR/97-1, September 1997.
[3] U.S. Census Bureau, cited by Dr. John H. Stevens in the 10.8.98 edition of *News*, First Presbyterian Church, Colorado Springs, Colorado.

at about one child per divorce. In mid-1997, about 19 million children (one in four) under the age of eighteen lived with only one parent.[1]

> In junior and senior high, I knew just as many kids with single parents as I did who came from "traditional" families (whatever that means). —Kate
>
> A person should marry another person because they know they're going to be with that person for the rest of their lives, so I think it's sad when two people have to get a divorce.—Ben
>
> Divorce is acceptable—is that reversible?—Eli

With or without us, our babies grew to be children. Then, while we elected presidents we would sooner have thrown eggs at when we first got the vote, our children turned into teenagers who seemed to feel as great a distance from us as we felt from our parents. We made cracks, then nagged, then yelled, then shook our heads disapprovingly, then gave up on them—everything we said we would never do. And it felt bad.

Actually, it *feels* bad. We're not done yet. Many of us have a good bit of child-rearing before us. The number of American kids under the age of eighteen reached 70.3 million in 1995.[2] Just to give you a point of reference, there were 69.9 million under-eighteeners in 1966.[3] That was a lot, but it was the top of the Baby Boom. The numbers are still growing this time, and many of them are ours.

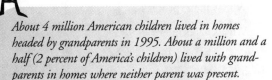

About 4 million American children lived in homes headed by grandparents in 1995. About a million and a half (2 percent of America's children) lived with grandparents in homes where neither parent was present.

—**U.S. Census Bureau**

University of California-Berkeley professor of public health, Meredith Minkler noted that many custodial grandparents are affluent and many are surprisingly young—grandparents in their late 20s who became parents as teenagers, whose children did too.

—**Los Angeles Times**

The rest of us have much work to do with our adult children.

> Most of our adult kids aren't hard to find. A lot of Boomers left home without going very far. Most of our kids never left home at all, or left briefly, then returned, some bearing the gift of grandchildren we now raise in part or in whole. That wasn't supposed to happen.

Even those who don't have drinking-age heirs in a bedroom down the hall seem to have plenty of unfinished business with their adult children. Again, I may be wrong, but I can't think of many people who have a clean slate with their offspring, grown up or not. I still have amends to make with Kate, and we get along about as well as any daughter and father I know.

Here's the thing. We can raise adults. We can rebuild bridges with our adult children and we can get it right the first time with the younger ones. Forgive the cliché, but it's not rocket science. It's relationships—which means it's both harder and easier. Rocket science depends on precision. Relationships depend on passion. I don't know anything about precision relationships and I don't anyone who does.

> People are essentially unreliable under stress. Sometimes people make apparently senseless choices. Folks choose self-sacrifice when they don't have to, or self-destruction when there's clearly a better way. There's nothing precise about it. What's behind those choices is pure passion.

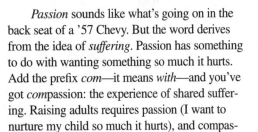

Passion sounds like what's going on in the back seat of a '57 Chevy. But the word derives from the idea of *suffering*. Passion has something to do with wanting something so much it hurts. Add the prefix *com*—it means *with*—and you've got *com*passion: the experience of shared suffering. Raising adults requires passion (I want to nurture my child so much it hurts), and compassion (I choose to share my child's suffering).

I don't know any painless way to raise adults. What I do know is that passionate and compassionate parents, teachers, coaches, and mentors tend to get the job done.

So, how bad do you want it?

Here's a brief exercise to keep the ball rolling.

🏃 Try to imagine three or four snapshots you could show someone to help them understand what your childhood and adolescence were like.

> Who is in the picture?
>
> What's happening?
>
> If you could add sound, what would we hear?
>
> What did you do because of that snapshot?
>
> What do you do now because of that snapshot?
>
> What don't you understand about that?

🏃 Try to imagine three or four snapshots that would help someone understand your child's life so far.

> Who is in the picture?
>
> What's happening?
>
> If you could add sound, what would we hear?
>
> What did your child do because of that snapshot?
>
> What does your child do now because of that snapshot?
>
> What don't you understand about that?

🏃 Don't take my word for it. What did you read here that's worth checking with a kid?

Canary in a Coal Mine

1.3

In our culture,

adolescents are

generally the first

to succumb to toxic

conditions.

Deep-shaft miners used to take tiny songbirds to work—probably still do in some places. The reason has less to do with bird songs than the fact that songbirds are delicate. This fact will be confirmed by any pet owner who ever found her feathered friend facedown on the newsprint. That domestic weakness is an asset in the mine shaft. The little fellas have tiny respiratory systems and remarkable but equally tiny brains. Said plain, toxic gases are sometimes released in deep mines—gases that kill. Songbirds keel over long before the fumes are deadly to humans. The birds are an early warning system. If the singing stops, everyone heads for the surface.

In our culture, adolescents are generally the first to succumb to toxic conditions. Look around. It's not hard to see that, for many kids, the song is over.

Much has been made of the increased rates of adolescent suicide. According to the National Center for Health Statistics, the rate of suicides among fifteen- to twenty-four-year-old Americans rose from 4.5 per 100,000 in 1950 to 13.8 per 100,000 in 1994—nearly 5,000 deaths by suicide that year.[1] These numbers don't include the widely held (though difficult to prove) belief among health care professionals that a disturbing percentage of accidental deaths—especially one-car accidents—are really suicides.

[1] U.S. Census Bureau, Vital Statistics Report, as of October 1998.
[2] Institute for Sexual Health, P.O. Box 162306, San Antonio, TX 78716.

It's only fair to note that the suicide rate in my generation was higher than our children in 1994: 15.3 per 100,000, nearly 13,000 deaths. Just thought you oughta know.
—U.S. Census Bureau, Vital Statistics Report

The toxicity in our culture can be measured by violent crime, lower achievement, higher rates of pregnancy, the percentage of America's children living in poverty, sexualized violence against and between children and adolescents, pandemic levels of sexually transmitted diseases (STDs), eating disorders and self-mutilation, addictive behaviors and drug dependency.

According to the Medical Institute for Sexual Health, 20 percent of American college women report having been manipulated or forced to have sexual intercourse against their will.[2]

I feel depressed just thinking about it.
But I won't be paralyzed. Not this time. I won't settle for ridiculous, quick-fix answers to complex questions.

FOR A SUMMARY OF DATA ON ADOLESCENT PREGNANCY AND STDS, SEE PAGE **84.**

> Let me be specific. "Just say no" is dumb. It was always dumb. Dumb, naive, moralistic, wishful thinking that, in my experience, made things worse. Way worse. Here's another one: "Kids are gonna do that stuff anyway; the best we can do is try to make it safe for them. That's why I let the kids drink at my house. At least I know where they are." Dumb.

> Just Say No doesn't work. You need something more than *no*.—Ben

> Just Say No is trite, over-used, ineffective, and the only answer some people can come up with.—Kate

> If someone tells you yes, no isn't the right answer.—Eli

> Just say no? Why?—Brian

I also won't put up with over-complicating the question. People who secure their jobs by creating the impression that all this is too difficult for lay people, do so with smoke and mirrors. I'm not saying there aren't *very* complicated issues in some cases. What I'm saying is, once we've heard the story behind the story, things usually make sense. When we can't make *any* sense out of things, and we're sure we really have the whole story, then it's time to call in serious reinforcements, and quick. But not until then.

[3] estimates from *Time*, June 9, 1997, p. 58; *Business Week*, February 15, 1999, p. 82.

Part of the mess we're in stems from something called *class diagnosis*. Class diagnosis is what happens when we think everyone in a group shares the same characteristics and problems by virtue of being in the group. It's not that class diagnosis is completely without basis, only that it's a stereotype, a short cut, an easy answer to a complicated question.

> Class diagnosis seems most dangerous to me in the hands of politicians and social scientists because some of them have the power to lock kids up or drug them or establish law enforcement standards that are hard on kids.

It was class diagnosis when I was young and they called my peers the *Me Generation*. We hardly had a chance to prove them wrong or right. They just assumed.

Class diagnosis happened again when marketeers jumped on Douglas Coupland's novel *Generation X*. They weren't trying to understand; they were looking for market share, trying to get their hands on the 125 billion dollars young Americans spend each year.[3]

Coupland said it was never about demographics or even a real generation. *Generation X* came from Paul Fussel's funny sociological book called *Class*. Generation X is people who don't fit into any generation because they won't fit in: A fifth column of people whose values run counter to the current culture.

IF YOU'D LIKE TO EXPLORE *THE STORY BEHIND THE STORY* RIGHT NOW, GO TO PAGE **112**.

Coupland wrote a eulogy for the term Generation X:

The problems started when trendmeisters everywhere began isolating small elements of my characters' lives— their offhand way of handling problems or their questioning of the status quo—and blew them up to represent an entire generation . . . . Around this time my phone started ringing with corporations offering from $10,000 and up to talk on the subject of How to Sell to Generation X. I said no. (The Gap asked me to do an ad. It was tempting, but I politely refused.) In late 1991, after both political parties had called to purchase advice on X, I basically withdrew from the whole tinny discourse.

And now I'm here to say that X is over.

—Details, *June 1995, page 72*

Yeh, fine. But the question remains: How do we sell them stuff?

I've been dismayed at lists of danger signs parents should watch out for in their children—lists that include things like:

- New, different friends
- Changes in eating or sleeping patterns
- Fatigue
- Weight gain or loss
- Lower achievement in school
- Changes in dress style
- Changes in musical taste
- Belligerence
- Spending large amounts of time alone behind closed doors

Sorry, but with the exception of radical weight gains and losses or precipitous drops in achievement, these changes are so typical of adolescence as to be normal. Can they signal the first step down the slippery slope to drug abuse? Yes. They can also mean the sudden discovery of snowboarding or basketball or country music.

Look, I'm as concerned about the country music problem as the next guy, but I'm not gonna panic because my kid comes home in a Garth Brooks T-shirt. There could be a perfectly innocent explanation. Like, "The dog ate my Nine Inch Nails shirt." I'll be danged if I'm gonna start World War III over a stupid T-shirt, however stupid the shirt may be.

Of course, I'm sad when parents miss clear signs of trouble. It means there's been a disconnect and that's never ever good news. I have friends who wish to God they'd paid attention to the storm clouds gathering in a child's life. I know other people who drove their children into the night because they panicked over a list of *symptoms* that was supposed to put them on notice but, mainly, put them on edge. I've seen a fifteen-year-old boy hospitalized and medicated because he consistently failed to keep his room clean and had a short temper (not violent, just short). I've seen several kids put on powerful drugs because they had trouble paying attention at school. I've seen adolescent girls praised endlessly for how good they looked until it became clear they were "cheating." Next thing they knew they were hospitalized for eating disorders, which they had and to which their families and friends and the whole freaking culture contributed by congratulating them every time they lost an ounce and criticizing them for anything less than the appearance of perfection.

And the hospital was supposed to sort through all that before the insurance ran out. Their moms couldn't even get the stink of vomit out of those girls' bedroom closets before the insurance ran out. The same goes for boys and anabolic steroids. Talk about craziness.

These days it's harder to get a kid into a psychiatric hospital because the insurance companies got wise to class diagnosis. But not before dozens of hospitals around the country made millions of dollars locking kids up for as long as the insurance would pay. Some of the treatments attempted to blend behavior modification (a Skinnerian process of resocializing based on deprivation and reward) with 12-step programs (a peer-based process of identifying, admitting, and surrendering out-of-control behaviors to a *higher power*). An unlikely combination since the two are virtually antithetical. A hospitalized kid, learning to beat the behavior modification system, found it easy to get friends to meet him at open 12-step meetings held in the hospital's community room. He got points from the hospital staff for going to the meeting and drugs from friends who infiltrated from outside.

Sounds like a win/win to me.

Wait, there's more. I've known kids hospitalized for eating disorders and more overtly suicidal behavior who accomplished much more than simply scoring drugs in a treatment facility. They learned to beat the treatment system, which is based on a simple scheme of rewards and punishments, in a matter of days. Some gained early release, not because they were better, but because they were better than the system and figured out how to say what their keepers needed to hear in order to sign the release papers. I even know a couple of kids who gained extended time in the hospital by relapsing at the right moment, so they wouldn't have to go home. I give them high marks for ingenuity and problem-solving.

Do you remember Abraham Maslow's Hierarchy of Needs? Maslow said people work from the bottom up, taking care of basic needs like food and shelter, before they get around to loving and being loved or self-actualization. It doesn't matter what you think about that because this has nothing to do with the Hierarchy of Needs. But it does have to do with Maslow, who also said, "When your only tool is a hammer, every problem looks like a nail."
That, in a nutshell, is class diagnosis.

The attractive thing about class diagnosis is this: It's easy. Neither the official nor unofficial kind requires much contact, dialog, or real analysis. It's all on the surface, so it's easy. It's also wrong. We resented it when they did it to us; our children resent it now. It isn't scientific—it isn't even rational. It certainly isn't fair.

Class diagnosis has a still uglier outcome: Self-fulfilling prophecy.

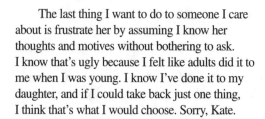

When we kept hearing how self-centered our generation was, a lot of us reached a point where we seemed to give in. Why wouldn't we? American business worked from the hypothesis that self-centered people could be bought. So they tried to buy us and, eventually, it worked. They were able to buy us, at least partly, because we bought into the stereotypes of our out-of-control appetites.

When our children hear how lazy, unmotivated, and disaffected they are, some of them reach a point where they seem to give in. Why wouldn't they? We don't ask, we just assume.

And you know what happens when we assume . . .

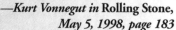

Those who graduate from high school or college this spring are not Generation X or Y, as envious middle-aged baby boomers have been pleased to tag them. They are as much Generation A as Adam and Eve were, as the middle-aged baby boomers, their parents, used to be.
—Kurt Vonnegut in **Rolling Stone,** *May 5, 1998, page 183*

The last thing I want to do to someone I care about is frustrate her by assuming I know her thoughts and motives without bothering to ask. I know that's ugly because I felt like adults did it to me when I was young. I know I've done it to my daughter, and if I could take back just one thing, I think that's what I would choose. Sorry, Kate.

Can you identify ways you think kids are the first to show the stress in our culture?

Where have you seen the negative effects of class diagnosis?

Have you indulged in class diagnosis yourself? With what results?

Don't take my word for it. What did you read here that's worth checking with a kid?

Toxicity

1.4

I don't believe our
problems stem from
exposure to drugs,
pornography, and
violence. That's
way too easy.

> Competition is the way to make sure I succeed in everything I do. If there's no one else, I can always compete against myself (or my image of myself).—Kate

> Most feel they're in the back or middle of the pack anyway.—Eli

> And another thing! If there's something I *really* won't put up with anymore, it's the notion— really it's a *belief*, held with special passion by religious folk who I think should know better— that the toxicity is all *out there* in society. You know who you are. You wanna quote the Bible at me? Come on! I'll quote right back.

> Whatever happened to "It's not whether you win or lose, it's how you play the game"?

The toxicity is not *out there*. I don't believe our problems stem from exposure to drugs, pornography, and violence. That's way too easy. I think the flow goes the other direction. Drugs, pornography, violence—the whole shootin' match—move from the inside out. They are symptoms of deeper issues. Exactly which issues is the subject of much debate in our culture.

Cheating and other shortcuts are no-brainers for most kids. In fact, many of them are genuinely surprised and confused when they get busted for arriving at the right place just because they got there the wrong way. College students can buy research papers and pay people to take tests for them because success is measured in grade–point averages more than learning. What's wrong with that?

> Of course, exposure to drugs, pornography, and violence sends the message that they're OK.
> —Eli

> Cheating is understandable and expected, if not approved of.—Brian

> The end justifies the means. "Ask my parent (not you of course, but metaphorically) how they got where they are—or just ask your local politician . . ."—Kate

> If appearances are what counts . . . and no one will know . . .—Eli

There's a lot of evidence that kids listen to adults before they listen to their peers.[1] You'd think this isn't true because of the mythology around peer pressure. The truth is, kids gravitate first toward older people who accept and value them and with whom they feel safe. If no one like that is around, then they look to peers for relationship, affirmation, and support. The upside of this is that caring adults help kids grow as whole persons. The downside is that what many adults care about isn't good for kids—or adults for that matter.

It's from adults that kids learn winning is everything and outcomes are more important than processes.

Adults teach kids that pain is bad. The whole system persuades kids to avoid pain at all costs

[1] See, for example, Robert Coles, *The Moral Intelligence of Children* (New York: Random House, 1997), pp. 5, 162-164; and George Barna, *Generation Next* (Ventura, CA: Regal Books, 1995), p.64.

or, should they be unfortunate enough to find themselves in pain anyway, to kill it decisively. Whole industries exist to combat pain quickly and effectively.

> Talk about mixed messages. "No pain, no gain" is marketplace sloganeering at its best. The application of this message is narrowly focused on skiing, skating, snowboarding, biking, hiking, climbing, surfing, sailing, and extreme variations on these themes. All of which are profit-making ventures for those who provide related services, facilities, and equipment. All of which are *followed* by messages for products that promise to manage the pain or enhance the gain. Somewhere a classroom teacher is saying "no pain, no gain" to motivate kids to read world history. I just know it.

Other enterprises, which appear to be dedicated to something else, are in fact part of the painkilling.

> You hear about the fight between Mothers Against Drunk Driving and Abercrombie & Fitch? The Mothers were all mad at A&F because, mixed in with the hot fashion statements, a Fall catalogue included directions for creative drinking games to replace your standard college beer binge. This is rich: teaching college students how to drink more creatively. Is that a for-credit course? Pass/Fail? As a bonus, the clothing catalogue included recipes for hard core cocktails like the "Woo-Woo" and "Brain Hemorrhage."

> Lonnie Fogel, an A&F spokesman, said, "The catalogue aims to be a chronicler of the American college experience." But they agreed to attach a sticker to the catalogue: "We don't want to lose anybody to thoughtlessness and stupidity. For some, part of college life includes partying and drinking—be smart and be responsible." And, hey kids: if enjoying too many Woo-Woos makes you woo-woozy, try lying down before you have a Brain Hemorrhage.[2]

In our culture, pain equals failure. Or it equals aging, which equals failure. So we self-medicate in order to succeed.

And so do our children.

> Pain is an unwelcome guest.—Brian

> Pain is a necessary but difficult part of life. Pain helps us experience joy more profoundly. Pain gives us depth as people.—Alice

> Pain just might make things better.—Eli

The problem is, much of the pain kids feel doesn't respond to over-the-counter drugs because it's more emotional than physical. I'm not saying emotional pain doesn't have physical manifestations. I'm saying analgesics won't make that ache go away.

But alcohol will. And nicotine will. And marijuana. And inhalants.

[2] I picked that up from The Ivy Jungle Network Campus Ministry Update (www.ivyjungle.org, August 1998.)

The prevailing sentiment about drinking is, "You gotta get drunk at least once." More and more that has to happen by age 16 or 17.—Kate

Drugs are all about peer pressure and vulnerability.—Eli

Drinking and drugs: two things I wish we could un-invent.—Ben

Drugs are frightening but intriguing at the same time. . . . I wonder what it feels like to be high. —Alice

In a different way, crack cocaine and crystal methamphetamine take the pain away fast. As do LSD and a list of other substances as long as my arm.

Stimulants, depressants, psychedelics . . . pick your poison. Add heightened levels of naturally occurring body chemicals like adrenaline and you've got a potent cocktail. Kids have those body chemicals in abundance. Adrenaline races to their hearts and muscles when they're excited or afraid, increasing strength and endurance. And when are kids *not* excited or afraid?

Kids live most of their lives in three states: excited, afraid, asleep. Sometimes all at once.

The list is not yet complete. Relational stimulants and depressants are as powerful as chemical reactions. You've seen both. You know people in-love-with-being-in-love who move from relationship to relationship in search of a romantic buzz, always hoping the next one will be permanent. You also know people who look for partners who will despise and dominate and punish them and who hang on to those abusers for all they're worth. That's not just a peer thing. Some kids will do anything to please or placate their parents, mentors, teachers, coaches, or employers. Including lying to spare those authority figures from disappointment. As upside-down as it seems to most adults, many kids see lying as a respectful, loving, sensitive act if it protects someone they look up to from unpleasant information. I can't imagine where they learned that.

And let's not forget about sex.

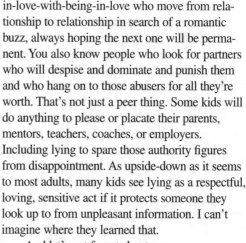

Can I just tell you how much pornography fries my bacon? I'd like to take those people for a long walk on a short pier. But I gotta be honest. I don't think it would make sex abuse go away. I have a blind buddy who's never seen a single picture, but he's as lusty as any man I know. I'm a pretty good judge of these things because *I'm* as lusty as any man I know.

And let's not forget about food.

My first year in college, I binged my way to a twenty-pound net gain, all of which I lost the next year. After college, I ramped up gradually until I weighed about fifty pounds more than when I reached physical maturity. Food, it seems, was to become my drug of choice: cheap, legal, and readily accessible. I already knew about food because my mother and several aunts were pushers. Plus, I grew up in a church where, whenever two or three were gathered together, there was food and plenty of it.

But my unhealthy relationship with food wasn't merely a question of abundance. I abused food because of its emotional impact. I ate when I was nervous, when I felt depressed, when I had something to celebrate, when I felt lonely or sad, elated or challenged. Food has never let me down. I may not be able to reason my way out of a difficulty, I may fail to make my point in a dispute, I may be afraid the lid's about to come off or the bottom's about to drop out. In any and every case, food makes me feel better.

> I think about food constantly; sometimes I plan my day around it! It's pretty unhealthy, I think. —Alice
>
> Food—Frustration—Ben & Jerry's (hey, it works for Ally McBeal).—Kate
>
> Mmm . . . —Eli

Does this mean that food is bad? No. It means good things can be used badly.

Before this collapses into an essay on addictive behaviors, let me return to the point. Let's see, what was the point?

Oh, right, the point is: Toxicity is not out there. It's an inside job. And in the parts that *are* influenced by outside forces, our kids listen to and learn from us first, before their peers. In many ways, they follow our examples to excruciating lengths. Only the details of their behavior are different.

On your best days, how do you tend to cope with stress and pain?

How do you tend to cope with stress and pain on your worst days?

On a scale of one to five, how well would you say you cope with pain and stress overall?

| 1 | 2 | 3 | 4 | 5 |

How do you feel about that number? Is it where you want to be? If so, how did you get there? If not, what do you think you want to do about that?

On his best days, how does your child tend to cope with stress and pain?

How does he tend to cope with stress and pain on his worst days?

On a scale of one to five, how well would you say he copes with pain and stress overall?

| 1 | 2 | 3 | 4 | 5 |

How do you feel about that number? Is it where you wish he was? If so, how do you think he got there? If not, what do you think you can to do about that?

Don't take my word for it. What did you read here that's worth checking with a kid?

30-Day Guarantee

2.0

Warning: If you think these are techniques and try to trick kids with them, I promise you'll fail.

My friend went to a career seminar with the intriguing title,

How to Get Rich, Working Half Days

> Oh good! Finally! This *must* be it. The part about the seven secrets to better parenting, the ten keys to more wholesome children, the One True Thing.

The opening line of the seminar was, "I'm going to tell you how to get rich working half days. The first thing you have to do is decide which twelve hours you want to work."

Right.

I thought long and hard about this. I read a shelf full of books. I worked with kids for two and a half decades. I lectured and led parents. I watched the best parents and the worst parents I know. Susan and I raised an adult. Here's the one true thing: There are no secrets, keys, or steps. There's just you and maybe your partner, and one kid. However many kids you have, you still have to raise them one at a time. Some kids are ready at three for what other children won't handle until five. Try one-size-fits-all parenting (the same goes for teaching) and it'll come out looking like class diagnosis as sure as I'm sittin' here. So, sorry, I - can't give you three easy steps.

I do have this: I have a 30-Day Guarantee.

I guarantee that if you do nothing for the next 30 days, things will get better between you and your kid, if the nothing you do is what we're about to cover.

Seriously. Some adult behaviors are so toxic, *nothing* is way better than something. I promise things will be much better if you commit yourself to doing nothing for the next 30 days.

- No Hijacking
- No Fixing
- No Bossing
- No Demanding
- No Shaming
- No Taming

> Do nothing? I can do nothing! Don't think I can't. Just the other day I was sitting around and you know what I was doing? Nothing. If it's nothing you want, you've come to the right guy. Bring it on kids, I'll just sit here and watch things get better.

In truth, doing nothing may be more difficult than it sounds. You may have to overcome some chronic bad habits. Or you may be a proactive type who grows impatient with doing nothing. So, instead of just not hijacking, fixing, bossing, demanding, shaming, or taming for 30 days, I'll suggest *something different* you can attempt if you think you're up to it.

- Don't *hijack—explore*
- Replace *fixing* with *collaborating*
- Quit *bossing* and begin *partnering*
- Stop *demanding*; start *affirming*
- Instead of *shaming*, pay *respect*
- Give up *taming* and offer *encouragement*

WARNING: If you think these are *techniques* and try to trick kids with them, I promise you'll fail. These are *relational habits* that grow from personal and interpersonal skills.

Just start with a radical commitment to do nothing. It's worth the effort. If you have it in you to do something different, all the better. But that's not the guarantee. The guarantee is, "Do nothing and get better results."

How does the notion of doing nothing for 30 days strike you? Why?

What could keep you from giving the 30-Day Guarantee a try?

Is there another adult you can ask to partner with you on the 30-Day Guarantee?

Hijacking

2.1

Hijackers assume kids will make the wrong decisions, or at least different decisions from those the adult would, which, of course, makes the decisions wrong.

Hijacking begins with the belief that I know you better than you know yourself. I'm certain nothing could make you happier.

This is what an awful lot of adults (not just a lot of awful adults) regularly do to the kids in their lives. Come to think of it, adults do it to each other and I don't know anyone—adult or child—who enjoys it even a little bit.

Hijackers assume kids will make the wrong decisions, or at least different decisions from those the adult would, which, of course, makes the decisions wrong. No matter how mature the youngster actually may be, she will feel childish at the hands of the Hijacker.

"Do you have your lunch money?" is an insult on the lips of a Hijacker because it means "I'm pretty sure that, left to your own devices, you'd starve. Remember that time you forgot your lunch money? You were hungry, weren't you? I wouldn't want to let you make that mistake again." There's very little chance the child will be hungry at the end of this exchange. She's probably had about all she can stomach.

Most people mean no harm when they hijack. The goal, after all, is to head off undesirable consequences. But Hijackers do much harm to their relationships and the self-esteem of those they care for. The underlying message of hijacking is: *You're helpless without me. You need me for the most trivial matters. I'm saying this for your own good. You'd lose your mind if I didn't hand it to you on the way out the door every morning. Never forget that. And, honey, have a good day at school.*

Hijacking fosters dependence instead of encouraging intelligent independence. The

Hijacker insists on looking after details like what to wear, what to eat, how to study, when to sleep and wake, and how, specifically, to get from point A to point B. Then, should the child make the mistake of relinquishing control in any of these areas, Hijackers blame them for not looking after the little things any fool can accomplish in his sleep. It's a dirty business, hijacking.

You don't understand! It's for his own good!

Blah, blah, blah.

No, really; he'd forget his head if it wasn't attached!

Not more than once.

Kids have an amazing capacity to learn new tricks. They don't allow themselves to get very cold or hungry or lost more than once without very good reasons. One very good reason, of course, is to get under the skin of a Hijacker. I see a lot of kids on their way to school without jackets. I often imagine the conversation that occurred on their way out the door.

Interior. Morning. Kitchen. An eleven-year-old boy runs a piece of bread around the rim of a jelly jar and chews thoughtfully, having decided toast is too much trouble. From another room we hear an adult voice.

Adult: Are you wearing your jacket?

There is silence in the kitchen. The adult speaks louder.

Adult: Are you WEARING your JACKET!

The boy speaks, his mouth full of bread.

Boy: Snot cold!

Adult: What? I said, are you wearing your jacket?

Silence in the kitchen. After a moment the adult hollers.

Adult: ANSWER ME!

The boy glances up at the clock. Indeed, he is not cold at this moment. He is tired of being yelled at from another room. In an instant the boy decides he will placate the one in the other room but, for reasons he hardly understands, he will not satisfy her. His voice rises with the patronizing tone he will use again fifty years in the future when explaining to his mother why she must eat her strained vegetables.

Boy: Mom, it's too hot to wear my jacket in here. Don't worry about it.

With that, the boy dips his finger in the jelly, rubs it on another piece of bread which he folds neatly in half, walks past his jacket and out the door into the cold, clear day of his youth.

Remember the 30-Day Guarantee. If, for a month, you steadfastly keep your mouth closed, your child will have to think about things you've been taking responsibility for. Since you won't have been—dare I say it?—*nagging* her, maybe she'll talk with you about her experiences in those matters. She may want to blame you because she forgot something. She may try to shift responsibility back to you. If so, you'll know your silence is starting to work. Don't give in to your need to be needed. Do this: Express your sympathy about whatever she forgot and, without moralizing, decline to take back responsibility. Each time you take responsibility for details your child could be covering, you leave something else undone. It may be something nonessential like working on your watercolors or something essential like getting yourself to bed at a decent hour. Any chance *your* personal health and development might be important to your child?

Instead of hijacking a kid's opportunity to learn intelligent independence, work on your watercolors. Go to bed on time. Remain engaged but don't hijack your child's need to develop responsibility. Keep doing this for a month and watch things improve.

Exploring

If doing nothing for a month doesn't satisfy, and you think you have the energy, become an Explorer rather than a Hijacker.

Hijackers assume they know what other people think and feel and where they're likely to end up without control. Explorers assume nothing. The Explorer seeks information only his child can provide but probably won't volunteer unless she is asked.

"Just a moment," someone is saying. "'Are you wearing your jacket?' is a question." Okay, you got me on a technicality. It is a question. But, it's a loaded question, so it's not a very good one.

Wayne Rice, director of the parenting workshop, *Understanding Your Teenager*, offers this simple definition of a good question:

A good question is one to which you don't have the answer.

I like that a lot and here's why: Most questions are tricks. Kids get used to being tested and set up by adults.

> The first time a kid gives an honest answer to a question like "What were you thinking?" he learns the question was rhetorical. He may not know what *rhetorical* means, but he figures out that giving honest answers to rhetorical questions is a bad idea.

After a while, most kids learn to be cagey, to avoid direct answers. They learn the art of misdirection and answering questions with questions.

Into this madness comes the Explorer. Instead of asking, "Are you wearing your jacket?" she asks something like, "Do you have everything you need for your day? What's the weather look like?"

Everything I need for my day . . . the youngster thinks. And if he's learned to think through his day in advance (a skill encouraged by this kind of question), he will run a quick diagnostic on his preparation for the day. *Jacket: Won't need it. It's cool now, but sunny with a high in the mid-sixties and only 20 percent chance of precip. Uh, let's see . . . Lunch: Eating in the lunchroom today, got money. What else . . . Got my books. Omigosh! I have a game after school!*

"Mom! I have a game after school! Can you pick me up?" The boy arranges for transportation at 7:20 A.M. instead of scrambling for a ride at 5:20 P.M. It's almost an afterthought that causes him to stuff his jacket into his gym bag on the way out the door. *After all*, he reasons, *it'll be after dark when I head home and the temperature really drops after sundown*. The whole process takes fifteen seconds.

I hear cynical laughter at the back of the room. Your child is too stupid to learn that kind of intelligent processing. Is that what you're saying? Of course not. Your child's other parent was a strong swimmer in a reasonably clear gene pool.

So, if you're not saying that, please hear what I'm saying: The way to teach your child these skills is to become an Explorer. When asking good questions becomes a habit with you, providing thoughtful responses will become a habit for your child. That's the way it works. If your child leaves your home without those skills and must learn them the hard way, she won't thank you for all the times your foresight kept her from freezing or starving. And if she ever reads this book, she'll be mad at you for hijacking her opportunity to learn important skills at a time when the cost of learning was relatively low compared to what it cost her to learn those things as an adult.

Becoming an Explorer with your child also offers a number of bonuses:

- First, asking good questions and listening carefully to the answers will help you discover the weak spots in your child's skill set. When you know what needs attention, it's not terribly difficult to figure out what to do next.
- Second, when you take your youngster seriously enough to ask questions you can't already answer, you're preparing him to let you in on a whole lot of other, deeper stuff. Pair this skill with the development of a sophisticated emotional vocabulary and you've got the raw material for a deep, lasting relationship with your child.
- Third, your child won't automatically expect that all adults are out to make her look stupid. Maybe she'll give other adults a chance to demonstrate their real intentions and not assume the worst. Of course, she'll find the worst is true of many adults. In that case, the contrast between how you treat her and how those other jerks treat her will make you look really, really good.

Why do you think hijacking is so attractive?

How do you feel when someone thinks he can read your mind?

Can you think of three questions you can ask about your child's week that you don't already know the answers to?

Can you identify an area where your child may be resisting you because of hijacking?

What stands in the way of becoming an Explorer with the children in your life?

Don't take my word for it. What did you read here that's worth checking with a kid?

TO JUMP STRAIGHT TO EMOTIONAL VOCABULARY, GO TO PAGE 141.

Fixing

2.2

Not wanting our
kids to experience
pain, many of us
rescue them from
their failures and
wrongdoings.

The line between actions and consequences is severely blurred for most kids because, by and large, they don't understand the general principle of cause and effect. They don't understand cause and effect because the adults in their lives come behind them to fix things when they screw up. The problem is complicated by idle threats and equally idle promises.

An example: "If you'll be a good boy at the store [whatever that means], I'll buy you a treat," is easily lost in the excuse: "It's too close to dinner; you'll spoil your appetite." Not fair. Sure, we have to be concerned for the kid's nutritional well-being. So we'd better take care not to make idle promises in exchange for compliant behavior.

"All right, that's *it!* One more word out of you and we're going *straight* home!" Really? You're going to load everybody onto the bus and go straight home? I'm not saying you shouldn't do exactly that if it fits the situation. But please don't threaten to do it if you know you can't live with the consequences of following through.

> If I say, "Stop nagging! You kids are killing me!" I should have the decency to die the next time one of them nags me. Otherwise, it's an idle promise.

More to the point is the fact that, not wanting our kids to experience pain, many of us rescue them from the consequences of their failures and wrongdoing. When they're young we easily replace a toy, carelessly lost or broken in anger, and shield the child from the cost of his actions. Later, we drop what we're doing to deliver an item, thoughtlessly left behind, so our middle-schooler won't suffer a loss of prestige or miss a meal or fail to turn in a paper on time. Still later, we cover a negligently overdrawn checking account or pay the traffic ticket and insurance increase resulting from a moving violation or foot the bill for a medical procedure aimed at rescuing our beloved children from a ruined life.

And they resent us for it. Maybe not in the moment, but soon and forever, until we make things right.

Fixers come in every size, color, and shape. Rich, poor, and right down the middle. Some fixing is done out of guilt by parents who are otherwise disengaged. I remember the sad outrage my young friends expressed after a classmate's suicide. The kid drove off the end of a bluff, much as Thelma and Louise would a few years later. But there was no one chasing this girl. The others couldn't believe her parents were so dense. She'd already totaled two vehicles in single-car accidents, but her father and mother just didn't get it. They dutifully replaced the second car with a third, sturdier one—the one she used to kill herself.

> That's probably an extreme case. Nothing like that probably ever happened in another family. Probably couldn't ever happen again.

Another kid I knew stacked her empty liquor bottles in the bedroom closet. From time to time, her mother cleaned them out without a word. The mom told me she wanted her daughter to know she knew about the drinking. What she didn't want was the confrontation. Of course, that inevitably came when the kid got so strung out she couldn't function any longer. When things finally unraveled, the girl said she couldn't understand why her mom ignored her for so long.

The stories multiply in my head.

An adolescent girl who tortured and killed frogs and insects to gross out her parents and friends around the family pool eventually killed herself. Everyone wondered why she was so angry. No one asked. Another came home from a trip to find all her laxatives and diuretics—the medicinal part of her anorexia—neatly arranged on her dresser. The girl put the drugs back in the closet and continued her eating disorder, feeling more alone than ever. Years of physical and emotional harm passed before she started ironing that out with her mom, woman to woman.

Fixing doesn't fix a thing. At best, it postpones the inevitable. At worst, it's deadly.

A couple of days ago, I killed a mouse. I didn't relish the task so I did it quickly. I did it because the mouse was caught in a trap someone else set; its back leg broke when the metal bar snapped shut.

The little guy was moving around pretty good on three legs, trying to get free, but I could see it wasn't going anywhere. My mind flashed to another mouse in another trap.

I didn't want that one inside either. That was the point of the trap. But it was moving about so convincingly that I took it outside, figuring it would hobble away. It seemed like a good fix. A couple of hours later I went out to be sure it got away. It

didn't. I found it convulsed in pain, swarmed by ants crawling in and out of its mouth and nose. I felt sick. I feel sick remembering it now.

So, a couple of days ago, I killed a mouse because there was no good fix. I didn't relish the task so I did it quickly.

Our kids can't afford to have us fix things for them. They may not be able to survive it. What they need is honesty, accountability, and decisive action.

If, for a month, you refuse to bail your kid out, he'll be surprised, then angry, then hurt—then he'll slowly begin to stop expecting you to fix things.

And, in case you were wondering, don't expect him to say thanks. At least not right away.

Collaborating

Instead of fixing, try collaborating. The Fixer follows an expedient path to short-term good. The Collaborator imagines a time when he won't be on hand to fix things or a circumstance too complicated to be simply fixed.

The Collaborator—who is also an Explorer—begins with questions designed to find out what the child knows. One of the great things about collaboration is that it's equally valuable in positive experiences or negative *learning* experiences. Kids can learn to repeat positive experiences and avoid negative ones. The collaboration is virtually the same.

Here are the three big questions for the Collaborator:

What? Why? How?

"**What** do you think happened?" is not a technique question, so don't get hung up on the wording. The words can vary: "What do you think happened?" or "Please tell me about it." or "What stands out for you from that experience?" Whatever words you use, you're inviting your child (or student or employee) to put a name on her experience. The subject might be a disagreement over a book or film or a lecture about a close call on the highway. Doesn't matter. What matters is hearing what the kid thinks she experienced.

"**Why** do you think it happened?" Once he's identified what seems to have happened, your kid is ready to assign meaning to the experience. The question is why, out of all the possible outcomes, did this one occur? "Why do you think you identified more closely with that character in the book than with the others?" tells the Collaborator and the child something neither may have known before they considered the question. "Why do you think you misunderstood your sister?" invites a consideration of why he heard something other than what she said. "Why do you think you overestimated the amount of gas in the tank?" calls for an assessment of decision-making skills and wishful thinking. All valuable processes.

"**How** do you think you could repeat this success [or avoid this failure]?" This is the money question. If a child can answer this question, the learning cycle is complete. Now she can take strategic action to repeat success or avoid failure.

She may or may not be emotionally prepared to take the action. Whichever, the Collaborator will have a chance to repeat the same process next time, celebrating success or commiserating with failure. In either case, if the child can answer the What? Why? and How? questions, she's a step closer to intelligent independence.

The beauty about collaborating is you don't have to do it forever. Eventually, you can help your child see what you've been doing (and why and how you do it). Then, in most situations, she can take over the process herself.

In more formal learning situations, I frequently ask the What? Why? and How? questions this way: "What's the most significant thing you heard or thought about in this session? Why do you think that's so important? How do you think you might apply that to your life?" When I teach kids this process, I make a guarantee: "If you answer these three questions at the end of every class session and reading assignment, you'll raise your grade by half a point to a point." I've made this promise for more than a decade, and I've never had to take it back.

You may have noticed these questions are centered on the child rather than the adult. There are two reasons for this. First, the Collaborator is asking a question she doesn't already have the answer to. Otherwise it would be a trap. Second, I've come to believe that people learn what they *can* learn—what they're prepared to learn—rather than what they're *supposed* to learn. It would be great if we all learned sequentially, one thing after another until we knew it all. That's not the case. Complex learning is more like putting together a jigsaw puzzle. It's non-sequential and associative. So, when a child is asked to describe his own perceptions of an event, his answers are correct by definition: *This is what I thought was happening. This is why I thought so.*

It may be that his perceptions are inaccurate—he thought the digital clock said 11:10 P.M. when it actually said 1:10 A.M. So he was shocked to find out he was two hours late. Is there reason to believe he falsified his story? If not, he needn't be punished for a misperception. That doesn't mean he won't still pay the price of a broken agreement. It's a judgment call.

Whenever we ask, "What do you think happened?" we get another view of our child's learning curve. We get to compare where we thought he was on the curve, with where he really seems to be, with where he's supposed to be.

That creates a matrix that's updated every time we process a significant event, whether positive or negative. And if we can effectively process a negative event, it's likely to become positive. That's what we call "learning from our mistakes."

🏃 Are you a Fixer? Why?

🏃 What's the most significant thing you read or thought in this chapter?

🏃 Why do you think that's so significant?

🏃 What do you think you might want to do about that?

🏃 Don't take my word for it. What did you read here that's worth checking with a kid?

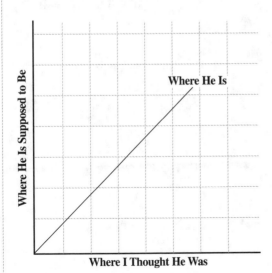

Where He Is

Where He Is Supposed to Be (y-axis)

Where I Thought He Was (x-axis)

Bossing

2.3

Nobody likes

to be around

bossy people.

Nobody likes to be around bossy people. Bosses know too much. They know how to do it—whatever *it* is—better than anyone else. They're impatient with those who do things differently. Bosses are a big pain in the behind.

No, give me that towel! You're not folding it right. This family has folded towels the same way for six generations: in thirds the short way, then in thirds the long way. How could you not know that? Note that "How could you not know that?" is in the form of a question. But is there anything in the context or tone of the question to make a child believe this parent is really an Explorer?

> **What really curdles my cream is that bossy people usually forget where they learned what they know.**

No, don't turn here, this is the long way! Just pay attention; I'll show you how to get there. The kid thinks, "Why don't I just let you drive? In fact, let me out here; I'll catch the next bus."

That's not the way to load the dishwasher. You can get more in if you . . . Oh, just give me the plate, I'll do it.

Okay.

> **If you've been bossing, please stop. Humankind will thank you. I promise.**

Partnering

The opposite of bossing is partnering. A Partner asks for help when she needs it, seeks insight from others, makes room for differences in style,

doesn't make a big deal out of things that don't really matter.

A Boss turns into a Partner when he decides his way isn't the only way. Or when he reaches the end of his rope. When there's too much work and not enough time. When he's sick or double-booked or just plain worn out.

When that time comes, the only question is whether anybody is left to partner with. The Boss may have done so much relational damage that no one wants to help. *Why put myself on the line for someone who's going to criticize me for not being him? He's already made it perfectly clear that I'm inadequate for the job.*

On the other hand, if I love my Boss, I may be willing to help when she really needs it. All she has to do is ask.

Asking for help, and really meaning it, spells the end of bossing. And most reformed Bosses never look back because partnering is way more fun, more inviting for everyone involved, more energizing. Partners learn to relish two extra minutes of drive time if that time can be used to build a relationship. Partners don't mind not getting every plate and glass in the dishwasher if it means standing next to a child and chatting while they wash the overflow dishes together. Simply put, Partners place more value on people than precision.

I'm not saying there's no place for the pursuit of perfection. I want a surgeon committed to zero defects in her team. But there's no place for *perfectionism* in human relationships. When we're talking about household chores or getting across town, if someone gets it wrong, nobody dies.

What's the big deal that's worth alienating our children over how the dishes get loaded?

Next time you realize you just freaked out over a detail that was, in the grand scheme of life, less than nothing, try being your own Collaborator. Take a moment and ask yourself:

- What just happened here? What did I say and do in front of my child? What message do I think he got from me?
- Why did I send that message? Why did that seem so important to me just then?
- How do I want to proceed from here? What do I want to communicate in the next thirty minutes? How do I want to handle myself next time something like this comes up?

Partnering is just plain better than bossing. When I partner, my kid becomes a participant, not just an observer. I want that. When I partner, my child learns new skills that prepare her for the future. I want that too. When I partner, I free up time to focus on other important things—like how I'm really doing in life.

Okay, I'm not so sure I want that. But it is what I need. The truth is, one reason I get bossy about details that really matter only to me (raising a simple task to the level of national security) is to divert myself (and you, I hope) from the truth about where I am and where I need to be.

You know, I really don't care for this line of reasoning. I'll forget about partnering if you will.

Is there a bossy person in your life? How do you feel about being bossed?

Is there a Partner in your life? If so, how do you feel about that person?

If you're prone to bossing, when are you most likely to do so? Why do you think that is?

What do you think would happen if you declined to boss for the next 30 days? Can you imagine any loss so critical that you couldn't recover from it?

What could keep you from partnering instead of bossing?

What's the most significant thing you read or thought about in this chapter?

Why do you think that's so significant?

What do you think you might want to do about that?

Don't take my word for it. What did you read here that's worth checking with a kid?

TO REVIEW COLLABORATION, GO TO PAGE **55**.

Demanding

2.4

When adults are

impatient in their

demands, kids

often bluff.

Demanding adults routinely criticize children for not being more adult. Their expectations are too high and too immediate for children to live up to. Their standards are unrealistic for the simple reason that they are adult standards.

There's nothing wrong with high standards if they're appropriate. Little kids can toddle, but most can't run. Hormone-ravaged young adolescents can use their heads, but most can't reason effectively all the time. Not yet. It's just a matter of time, health, and training.

> I never heard an adult criticize a toddler because she couldn't run. I guess there's something about the size and shape of those little bodies that tells us it's too soon to expect that. Maybe there's something about the size and shape of adolescent bodies that fools us into thinking they're more complete than they really are.

Adolescents are stuck in the middle—part child, part adult. They can be startlingly grown-up one minute and so maddeningly childish the next. I once interviewed an alcoholic fourteen-year-old in her bedroom. She told stories of alcohol-induced blackouts, while in the background the camera picked up cuddly stuffed animals on a shelf. Both were true expressions of her life at that moment.

This is why the state of Florida required extensive driver education and testing before entrusting me with a machine capable of hurtling down the highway at speeds in excess of eighty miles an hour. Okay, it was a 1957 Karmann Ghia with a top downhill speed of fifty on a straightaway—had there been a downhill straightaway in those parts. But you get the point. We require evidence of reasonably well-developed decision-making skills in middle-adolescents before we hand them the keys.

And we have a blanket, though ineffective, prohibition on the consumption of alcoholic beverages by children and adolescents.

> I'll never forget our crusade to lower the drinking age to eighteen. The reasoning was so clear: *We're old enough to fight and die for our country, but we're not old enough to do so under the influence of alcohol? C'mon!* Looking back, I don't think we were old enough for either. If you ask me, nobody under the age of forty should be allowed to perform military service. I'm willing to consider a drinking age somewhat lower than forty.

It's not that adults can't and don't get upside down with the bottle. It's that almost any kid will get upside down if he drinks because his body chemistry is immature and subject to devastating effects from alcohol.

The same goes for sex. I can think of a number of reasons to delay sexual involvement, one of which has nothing to do with emotions, relationships or morality: Immature vaginal tissue makes adolescent girls susceptible to pelvic inflammatory disease if they engage in vaginal intercourse. The more sexual partners they have, the more likely they are to suffer cervical cancer. They look all grown up, but they're not.

It's a bind. Because kids look grown up, adults demand grown-up perceptions and skills from them. The kids would like to deliver; they just can't. When adults are impatient in their demands, kids often bluff. Smoking cigarettes, drinking at parties, driving fast, accelerated sexual behavior—these all may be as much about bluffing as anything else.

There's an ol' boy in Alcoholics Anonymous, name of Clancy. Clancy says he had his first drink as a boy because the men said to join them and seemed to assume he would. He says he kept drinking for the next thirty years because drinking made him *feel* like other men *look*. That's bluffing.

Consider this: By the time kids are paying much attention, most parents have specialized to a point where their kids seldom see them fail. One parent balances the checkbook because the other isn't so good at it. The adults divvy up cooking, laundry, household repairs, shopping, extended family matters—everything, in fact—along lines of competence and comfort.

My profound sympathies if you're a single parent. You don't get to specialize. I can't imagine it's easy. But a lot of people are proving it's possible, and being single may give you the context to help your child see that no one is omnicompetent— nobody can do everything. Consider how to demonstrate trial-and-error learning to your child in areas where adequacy is the best you can muster. You may have that opportunity even if you're not single. Neither my wife nor I ever showed much aptitude in financial dealings. After decades of shame about that, I worked to attain a level of adequacy that I am moderately not dissatisfied with. I did this in plain view of our adolescent daughter, who seems to be more clever than either of us, due, I think, to a recessive gene in her mother's DNA. The important thing is that none of us is bluffing about our financial wizardry these days, so everyone is reasonably understanding of mistakes and wildly enthusiastic about successes.

Single, married, smart as a whip, dumb as dirt—we start from where we are. What else can we do? The nice thing is, when we do our best with what we have, our kids get a realistic peek into adulthood. And that ain't all bad.

In my estimation, demanding more than children can possibly deliver is more toxic than the risk of underchallenging them. In a reasonably healthy environment, kids will rise to life's challenges. They want to learn and grow because learning and growing are stimulating and fun. But real learning and growth are retarded in an overly demanding environment in which failure isn't tolerated. If failure isn't acceptable, trial and error are thrown out as a learning strategy and kids resort to compliance, docile repetition, and playing it safe. What could be more boring and less challenging than that? There's got to be a better way . . .

Affirming

I'm recommending that you refuse to be demanding for the next thirty days, just to see what happens in your relationship with your child. If you have the imagination and energy for it, affirming is better by far than just *not* demanding.

Affirming looks at a behavior or a process and responds with a constructive, concrete endorsement: "You did that well. I admire your work. Congratulations on a job well done." Affirming how a child performs isn't connected to whether she is nice, pretty, smart, or good. Affirming is more objective than that. It's also more specific. "Golly, you're really fast!" isn't nearly as good an affirmation as "Golly, you sure ran a good race! Tell me when you knew you had it won" or "Golly, you sure ran a good race! Can you tell me how you knew when to start your sprint at the end?" Affirming begins with honoring excellence. It continues with inviting interaction.

Affirming takes place independent of outcomes. A child doesn't need to win a race to be affirmed for her skill and dedication as a runner. So affirming is more realistic than demanding (on one end of the spectrum) and praising (on the other end). In this case, both extremes are unhealthy.

Demanding —— Affirming —— Praising

Consider two models of learning: one built on *orthodoxy* (the right word), the other on *orthopraxy* (the right practice). The model that depends on orthodoxy holds that students will *do* the right things once they've *learned* what things are right. The model that relies on orthopraxy holds that students will *learn* the right things once they *do* them and prove them right. Each model has its place.

> Lemme see if I've got this straight: Multiplication tables, alphabets, and telling jokes depend largely on orthodoxy. Striking a fair deal, writing a good letter, and being funny depend on orthopraxy. Naming the organs in the abdominal cavity is a matter of orthodoxy. Finding them by touch is a matter of orthopraxy. Is that right?

Most of the things parents teach their children are less about orthodoxy and more about orthopraxy. If you homeschool your kids, you'll do well if you master both learning models. Personal skills, relational skills, social skills, decision-making, problem-solving—these are learned in the process of trial, error, correction, training, and retrial. Consequently, parents are in a unique position to celebrate the learning process by affirming each trial, using failure as the context for correction and training, and applauding the next attempt.

When will you have a better chance to teach a child how to clean the kitchen than when he is four years old and eager to help? Why not put away the good dishes and sharp knives and let the little guy lend a hand? His attention span guarantees he won't help for long in the beginning, and he needn't be criticized for losing interest. Instead, acknowledge and affirm every effort as specifically as possible. "Thank you for helping me clear the napkins from the table" is better than "You're such a good boy to help Daddy clean the kitchen," when what the child did was clear napkins from the table.

In fact, here's how you'll know if you're trying too hard with affirmation. Affirming looks at an action and offers soberly generous appreciation. If you overstate the affirmation, you're trying too hard. If you turn affirming into praising, you're *really* trying too hard.

Praising makes artificial connections between an action and the worth of the person. That's serious business.

Think about it: A kid brings home a decent report card. The affirming parent says, "Good job! Congratulations! You must have worked hard to earn those grades—is that true? Tell me what it took to get these grades." And the two of them are off on a learning exercise that reinforces the processes that led to the child's success. That process may also uncover a class in which the child is underchallenged and lead to an exploration of effective ways to up the ante in that subject.

Another youngster brings home the same report card to a parent who settles for praising instead of affirming. She says, "You're so smart! I'm so proud of you! Kids, look how smart your sister is! Wow! All A's! Look at it close, Preston. It's just got the one letter, so I know you can read it. I think you could all learn something from this."

Indeed.

The kids have learned that a good report card is its own reward. Process means nothing, outcome is everything. Therefore, Preston will hide his next report card if it's not up to par. And Preston's sister, the smart one, will be tempted to cheat rather than risk bringing home a less-than-perfect report. She may or may not know the secrets of her own success. Her teachers may or may not have the insight and time required to draw out her description of the dedicated energy and imagination it took to earn the grades she brought home. If nobody brings that out, it's magic. She won't know how to repeat it if she doesn't know how it happened in the first place.

While I'm on this little rant about praising, let me note that much praise is offered for things children have nothing to do with. *You're so pretty! My, you're a big boy! Look at those beautiful blue eyes!* These are Acts of God. Children who get praise for things outside their control tend to become suspicious of people and nervous about their own worth. It's a particularly harsh setup for women whose looks will change radically over time. If the girl's self-esteem was anchored in being pretty, the woman's self-esteem will suffer when she is no longer girlishly attractive.

Later that evening, Preston's parent decides to make amends: "I'm sorry I hurt your feelings, Preston. You're a sweet boy. We can't all be as smart as your sister." Poor Preston. How can he improve his learning process if the only secret to success he knows is becoming his sister?

Can you recall an adult who demanded the wrong things from you when you were young? How do you feel about that?

Can you identify ways in which you're tempted to demand the wrong things from a child in your life? What contributes to that kind of temptation?

Can you recall an adult who affirmed you when you were young? How do you feel about that?

Have you seen praising substituted for affirming? If yes, what were the long-term results?

Take a moment to consider some area where you might legitimately affirm your child. Is there anything that would keep you from doing that?

What's the most significant thing you read or thought about in this chapter?

Why do you think that's so significant?

What do you think you might want to do about that?

Don't take my word for it. What did you read here that's worth checking with a kid?

Shaming

2.5

There's no reason to belittle a kid because he hasn't gotten to the part of the training where he knows better.

No one knows anything he didn't learn.

That's not a theological statement, in case you're looking for offenses against that form of political correctness. I will be happy to discuss innocence and depravity in another context. Meanwhile, adults are acting unreasonably if they humiliate children because the youngsters haven't yet learned adult things.

> **It may be worse. Some adults hold kids in such contempt, they're not just being unreasonable, they're being mean. The message is: If you don't know what I know, there must be something wrong with you.**

Stephen Glenn and Jane Nelsen call this *adultism* in their book, *Raising Self-Reliant Children in a Self-Indulgent World*:

> The language of adultisms is: "Why can't you ever? How come you never? Surely you realize! How many times do I have to tell you? Why are you so childish? When will you ever grow up? Did you? Can you? Will you? Won't you? Are you? Aren't you?"[1]

I have a confession: I've been that guy, most notably (though, not exclusively) in my own home. When our daughter, Kate, stood at the edge of adolescence, she seemed a bit, let's say *unbalanced*. It didn't last long, but the hormone bath her body gave her brain made Kate unstable for a few weeks. One night I marched into her room and, using language I don't use with anybody, told her we wouldn't be putting up with her *nonsense*.

The shock and pain in Kate's eyes broke my heart because I could see I had just broken hers. I fled her room in a fit of self-loathing. I was particularly ashamed because my day job at the time was working with adolescents. I knew plenty about puberty. But I forgot everything I knew when my own daughter got a little cranky. I viewed her with contempt for not being able to surf the hormonal tide surging through her body. I should've been flogged.

When I apologized, Kate readily forgave me and I believe she did her best to forget my meanness that night. Whether there's a scar from that slashing attack, I can't say for sure. I'm grateful she didn't repay contempt with contempt.

Shaming is a context where the interrogative form doesn't necessarily indicate an honest question. The words, "What were you thinking!?" can be asked in a tone that conveys a message so humiliating that the person on the receiving end, if he responds at all, can respond only one way: "I don't know." Anything else is just asking for it.

"I don't know" may well be an honest answer.

> **The toddler who sticks his finger in a light socket isn't thinking about much of anything; he's just poking around. At least I wasn't thinking about much of anything. But I still remember the moment I made contact. It occurs to me now that I already associated pain with punishment because my emotional response to that shock was guilt. Hmm . . . More therapy?**

[1] H. Stephen Glenn and Jane Nelsen, *Raising Self-Reliant Children in a Self-Indulgent World* (Rocklin, CA: Prima Publishing/St. Martins Press, 1989), p. 91.

The college student who overdraws her checking account, the young driver who ruins a truck transmission doing reverse donuts in a muddy field, the ten-year-old who uses steel wool to clean a silver serving tray—they weren't thinking about messing up, that's for sure. Their actions made sense at the time, however dumb they may look now.

So why shame them further? There's no reason to belittle a kid because he hasn't gotten to the part of the training where he knows better.

One other thought: Shaming sets kids up for undue influence from outside sources. That influence ranges from the dreaded peer pressure to overtures from the twenty-two-year-old man who wants a date. The reason for the setup is that shaming moves a child's point of reference outside her own cognitive understanding to someone else's point of view. If a parent builds a convincing case that the child is stupid and cites as evidence that the child doesn't know what the parent knows, then the next logical question in the child's mind is, *What else don't I know?* At which point he is easy pickin's for anyone who wants to exploit him.

Children who are shamed grow up to have sick relationships with their parents and others. They become people-pleasers and liars. I know this because it takes one to know one.

My mother, sweet woman that she is today, was an accomplished Shamer for many years. If I did anything unconventional, she would look scandalized and say, "Jimmy! Be ashamed!" She may have been half-kidding, but I took her advice all the same. And my father had a staggering capacity for shaming. I remember two occasions just a few months apart.

We were in the car, going downtown for something or other, and my father was doing a slow burn. Finally he vented: "Why aren't you wearing a shirt?" I was surprised and embarrassed by the question because I had chosen my wardrobe very carefully. This was 1966 or '67 and an acrylic crewneck sweater without a shirt was just about as groovy as anything could be—at least in my prep-driven neighborhood. My dad didn't see it that way. Maybe he thought folks would think he couldn't afford to buy me a shirt. He said, "People will see you like that in public. You're gonna ruin every damn reputation I have."I said nothing.

A few months later I spent the night with my closest friend, a smallish kid who was as brainy and funny as I wanted to be. When my father arrived to pick me up at Scott's place and found us wrestling, I could sense his disapproval. When we got in the car he said, "You shouldn't be playing with a little guy like that; a big ol' boy like you! People will think you're fairies." Yikes, Dad! What were you thinking?

Here's the thing. Guilt is the appropriate blush that says I did something wrong, I should make it right. Shame is a deeper blush that says I *am* something wrong and I can never be made right. I was well into my thirties before I started to recognize shaming for what it is. Shaming is a lie.

Respect

As fun as shaming is, it's not nearly as fun as mutual respect.

I had an uncle, several teachers, two youth-workers, and a coach who treated me with extraordinary respect. They listened to me and took my ideas seriously. They gave me training and responsibility. My uncle helped me learn to mow lawns before I was allowed to touch anything at home with a motor attached. My English teacher encouraged me to think outside the box and helped me learn to sort my thoughts and express them directly and economically. My coach helped me learn to think and communicate under pressure.

Respect isn't empty-headed acceptance of any and all behavior. Respect grows from the acknowledgment that all of us are in *process*. We've learned everything we know so far including the fact that we have quite a bit more to learn. Respect acknowledges that what's obvious to one person may not be a bit obvious to someone else and that's an acceptable place to begin the conversation. Shaming is a monolog. Respect is a dialog.

And isn't that what life is all about, the ability to go around back and come up inside other people's heads to look out at the damned fool miracle and say: oh so that's how you see it!? Well, now, I must remember that.
—**Ray Bradbury, quoted in an e-mail from my friend, Eric Johnson**

The surest way for me to show respect is to ask honest questions and listen carefully until, whether or not we agree, the other person tells me I really understand.

- Have you ever been shamed? How do you feel about that?

- Have you ever shamed a child? How do you feel about that?

- How do you feel toward people who respect you?

- How do you feel when you treat a child with respect?

- What's the most significant thing you read or thought about in this chapter?

- Why do you think that's so significant?

- What do you think you might want to do about that?

- Don't take my word for it. What did you read here that's worth checking with a kid?

Taming

2.6

If we teach our
children to eat,
drink and be merry
for tomorrow they
may die, they may
grow up fat, drunk,
and surprised to
be alive.

We live in a world of lowered expectations.

As a kid I was taught to believe that any boy could grow up to be president and, I suppose, any girl could grow up to be that president's mistress. Don't hit me; that's the America where I grew up. In fact, quite a few baby women grew up to prove that a woman's place is in the House, and in the Senate. They grew up to be governors and judges and attorneys general. Not bad for people who couldn't vote at the turn of the last century.

I wonder what my daughter will see in her lifetime.

The people we call Generation X were raised to believe they'd be lucky to have a half-decent job and afford a house and a car. Of course, in the global scale of things, this expectation doesn't exist. Most earthlings never expect to own the roof under which they sleep nor travel on anything but public transportation. But things have been different on this continent.

North Americans have surfed the economy like California long-board riders—wiping out big time in the thirties, then catching a succession of big waves in every decade since the forties. As I write these words, Wall Street is dragging itself to the beach after a bone-crunching face plant. Who knows? As you read this, the Dow may be at 5,000. Or it may have passed 15,000. What seems clear is that another set of waves is always forming. When the U.S. economy tanked in 1987, we heard dire predictions about our children's prospects. They would be the first generation of Americans who failed to improve their lives compared to the generation before them. That felt very true for about five years. Then the U.S. economy took off like Moody's Goose and everybody was better off, at least in the short run.

Short-run thinking has long-run results. If we teach our children to eat, drink and be merry for tomorrow they may die, they may grow up fat, drunk, and surprised to be alive. Then they have to figure out how to pay for the rest of their lean, sober years. If we teach our kids Spartan frugality because the wolf is at the door, they may grow up stingy and afraid, waiting for the next Depression, stockpiling food and weapons in vintage 1962 fallout shelters because the next crash will make the last one look like a short paycheck.

Mainly, I think, we teach our children nothing. By default, they learn their lives are none of their business. They learn that market forces they can't hope to understand control all our destinies. So why bother?

There's a note of realism in that. Life may spin out of control; things may get worse before they get better.

Things may even get worse before they get much, much worse. Don't bet the farm on a sure thing because there are no guarantees and every man must take his own pig to market. Whatever that means.

The trouble is, mixed with the realism is a note of fatalism that suggests there is no value to hard, intelligent work. Who was it who said, "The harder I work, the luckier I get"? Ah, it was Carl Karcher, the founder of Carl's Jr. restaurants, recalling how he built a fortune from a $300 hot dog stand. In his seventies and several million dollars in personal debt after fending off a hostile takeover, Karcher was busy plotting the repayment of those loans and the next wave of his company's fortune.

As Karcher nears the end of his working life—probably not more than a decade or so to go before he retires—a good number of twenty-something Americans are building fortunes the same way he did: tireless effort and enlightened trial and error. Slackers? I think not. Some of the most spectacular Initial Public Offerings in history were propelled by the work of men and women not yet thirty years old. Someone forgot to tell them they couldn't make it. Or maybe they ignored the message.

> I no longer believe any boy can grow up to be president. I do believe this: If you think you can, you might. If you think you can't, you won't.

Why tame our children's wild dreams?

Encouraging

Instead of taming our children's aspirations, why not encourage them? The verb *to encourage* means to put courage *in*. A line in the Bible says we ought to encourage each other to *love and*

good deeds. I really like that. There's so much to discourage our children—to take courage out of them. That's why I like Junior Achievement, the economic education agency that puts ordinary business professionals in classrooms to help kids learn about their place in the economy. And it's why I love Compassion International, the child development agency that creates hope for kids by training them to live well and to make a living wherever they are in the world.

Teachers are in a position to encourage kids. Youth workers, mentors, coaches, service industry employers, grandparents, law enforcement officers, entertainers, neighbors—we're all in positions to encourage. The big question is, Do we have courage to spare?

Remember, kids don't want to be pandered to any more than we do. If we offer false courage because we don't have a surplus of the real thing, they'll hammer us for it.

Here's an uncomplicated skill to help your child understand where to look for encouragement. I don't know whose metaphor this is. I first heard it from my friend, Paul Franklin. Paul said each person we meet is either a *fueler* or a *drainer*. Drainers *take* because they have nothing to give. Fuelers *give* because their tanks are full and they're generous with the surplus. In a lifetime, most of us will play both roles, depending on our circumstances. Along the way, some people turn into chronic drainers. It doesn't mean they're particularly bad people. But they're stuck. People who masquerade as fuelers may also become drainers because they need to be needed. These people manufacture crises wherever they go, further draining everybody they try to help.

To figure out where we are at a given moment requires skillful self-assessment. To recognize the influence of individuals in our lives requires answering three simple diagnostic questions.

- When she leaves, am I usually fueled or drained?
- What does she do that fuels or drains me?
- In light of that, how should I manage my interactions with her?

This is not rocket surgery. I'm learning to ask these simple questions and I'm a chronic people-pleaser. If I can learn it, any normal, reasonably stable person from about the age of ten on can master it.

And if I can learn to recognize how I am fueled or drained, I can learn to fuel my daughter, my wife, my extended family, my coworkers, friends, total strangers I meet on airplanes and . . .

Do you know what it feels like to have significant people try to tame your aspirations?

Who are the consistent drainers in your life?

Who are the consistent fuelers?

What's the most significant thing you read or thought about in this chapter?

Why do you think that's so significant?

What do you think you might want to do about that?

Don't take my word for it. What did you read here that's worth checking with a kid?

YOU CAN GO TO PAGE **133** FOR MORE ON SELF-ASSESSMENT.

Culture Soup

3.0

It's all about treating

kids humanly—

that's hard, selfless

work that has

nothing to do

with magic.

If parents, teachers, mentors, youth workers—all of us who nurture kids—learn to really, really listen, kids will tell us most of what we need to know to understand them. And raise them better.

What they'll describe, and what we can see if we look hard enough, is the cultural soup they're in. It's not our soup, exactly. But it's like our soup, with its own distinctive flavor. You may or may not like it. You may find it too salty for your taste or too pungent. Be that as it may, it's not your soup.

I've tasted this unusual blend of ingredients in every part of the country, from Miami to Anchorage, from Long Island to Long Beach. I find the same flavors among ethnic and socioeconomic groups that appear to have very little in common. I'm convinced that learning to appreciate this distinctive recipe leads to a deeper, more generous appreciation of individuals who are in this particular soup.

> Or not. Some adults are so uncomfortable they just wanna skip a generation. *Do we really have to deal with these kids? Can't we just ignore them and hope they'll go away?* Believe me, ignore them and they *will* go away.

❧

There's nothing particularly scientific about these observations if you're looking for hard data. Statistical abstracts are, for my purposes, interesting details in a larger picture. What I've been staring at all these years is a *gestalt*, the big picture of growing up in this culture. I'm interested in

1. Peter L. Berger, *Invitation to Sociology* (Garden City, NY: Anchor Books, 1963), pp. 23-24.

what the larger picture tells us about our children. My training (such as it is) is sociological, so I've compiled this list of cultural ingredients over two and a half decades of what sociologists call *participant observation*—becoming a fly on the wall. Since 1972 I've spent a lot of time hanging out with kids at school, at church, at the mall, on road trips. Often, I slip under the radar to observe things that can only be seen up close. And I've interviewed hundreds of adolescents, led hundreds of groups, listened to scores of parents, and mediated dozens of family disputes. I won't claim for a moment that I'm a disinterested observer. I do claim to have stepped away from my biases, suspending my personal agendas in an effort to understand and respond to things as they *are*, not as they're supposed to be.

> *It can be said that the first wisdom of sociology is this—things are not what they seem. . . . People who like to avoid shocking discoveries, who prefer to believe that society is just what they were taught in Sunday School, who like the safety of the rules and maxims of what Alfred Schuetz has called the "world taken for granted," should stay away from sociology.*
>
> —*Peter L. Berger* [1]

I was a college student when I started this process—still adolescent myself. Over time I became an advocate for kids, representing their interests, culturally and individually, to adults in churches, at schools, in newspaper and magazine articles, and with community groups. I suppose

I became an advocate for adults too, helping kids understand their parents, teachers, pastors, coaches, and employers.

What's just ahead in *Raising Adults* reflects all that. Where I have it, I've cited corroborating evidence from other sources. And I've taken pains to check my work with kids, indirectly and directly. My adolescent and twenty-something reviewers are giving me the thumbs-up.

There's a positive and a negative side to each ingredient in the cultural soup. And there's a corresponding adult action or reaction—an *if/then* relationship—that tends to encourage positive outcomes. These are specific actions and reactions to enhance the assets and limit the liabilities: *If* kids display this or that characteristic, *then* we might act (or react) in this or that manner to help them grow.

There's no magic in this process. In fact, it's all about treating kids humanly—that's hard, selfless work that has nothing to do with magic.

How do you respond to the desire some people have to skip a generation?

In the past, where have you found things were not as they seemed?

Are there any ways in which you suspect the "world taken for granted" may not be the real deal?

Sophisticated Innocents

3.1

Most of our kids never knew a day without a Walkman, a VCR, a personal computer, or MTV. To borrow from Donald Tapscott, they *grew up digital*.

Has there ever been a generation of children with greater access to information, technology, or culture?

Most of our kids never knew a day without a Walkman, a VCR, a personal computer, or MTV. To borrow from Donald Tapscott, they *grew up digital*. It's in their blood.

I think kids know too much to put their *faith* in science—they've already seen that get upside down more than once—but they *rely* on technology.

> For sure we rely on technology, but is it sophistication that prevents us from putting our faith in science? It could be apathy, a misinformed self-reliance, or something else along those lines. —Alice

As a class, they're as comfortable on the Internet as we are on the telephone—and just about as uncomfortable without it.

Sure it's a generalization. But not much of one. Of course, there are kids who don't have a telephone in their apartment. They make calls on a pay phone at the convenience store, maybe paying with a prepaid phone card—and already it's a more complicated transaction than our grandparents experienced when dialing zero or clicking the receiver to raise an operator. On the other end of the scale are families with dedicated fax/modem lines to enable their Internet wanderings without tying up their phones. Kids don't even think about the technology. They don't have to; it's *transparent*.

> Isn't transparency what sophistication is about? When something becomes so ordinary I don't have to think about it. And if I don't think about it, it really *is* a no-brainer. Sometimes that's good (*breathing* comes to mind). Other times, not so much. Take *content* for example.

Or take culture.

Our kids are multicultural in ways that would have shocked everybody but the children of missionaries, military brats, and the wealthiest kids of my generation. I think that's good. There's no turning back from globalization and I don't want to. One Planet, One People, and all that.

Our youngsters travel farther and more frequently than any generation before them. And it's not just that we can afford it; we can afford it because travel is cheap compared to when we were kids. Our kids are, Douglas Coupland said, "global teens."

The world comes to them as well. And not just Europeans (our great grandparents experienced that). These days, kids meet Asians, Central Americans, Africans, people from everywhere. Every major city has ethnic ghettos. More and more Americans are moving from those ghettos to the suburbs; many of those ghettos are suburban; more and more immigrants bypass ghettos altogether. Our children are exposed to music, clothing, culture, and marvelous food from everywhere.

And, because of television, everyone sees the news from everywhere, good and bad, in a matter of hours, if not minutes, if not live.

American kids meet exchange students from around the globe; many study in other cultures themselves. The more exposure kids have to people in the subcultures that border their own, and the earlier that exposure comes, the more naturally they build relationships that cross boundaries.

But that doesn't mean kids *understand* other cultures. There's every indication they don't. Xenophobia is alive and well; racism isn't dead (although it's sick). In 1998, Camille Cosby wrote an editorial in *USA Today*, saying the murderer of her son, Ennis Cosby, was taught to hate brown-skinned people after he immigrated to this country at the age of ten. Some people were mad at Ms. Cosby for saying so. But no one presented compelling evidence to dispute her point.

> Think about it: If a kid does manage to build a real cross-cultural relationship, his elders are likely to have a hissy fit of Shakespearean proportions—especially if there's (horrors!) romance involved. "I mean, don't get me wrong; I have nothing against <u>fill-in-the-blank.</u> But you know how they are about sex . . ."

How do we help children learn to observe and understand and value the content of other cultures? For that matter, how do we help kids learn sophisticated skills to understand and evaluate the content of their own cultures?

> For example: Take the media . . . please.

The media are neutral delivery platforms. There's nothing inherently moral about a computer or a film projector. It's the content that makes the difference. Trouble is, a lot of kids encounter content without assessing its value.

Especially sexual and linguistic content. Most kids are sophisticated in ways that would make their grandparents blush. There's nothing they won't see or hear sooner than later. We'd be hard-pressed to find a culture that exposes its children to more or protects them less.

> *By the time he's seven, the average American child has seen more shocking sexual images than his great grandparents saw in a lifetime.*
> —**H. Stephen Glenn, in a speech to the National Youthworkers Convention, circa 1988**

Ditto violence, drugs, and profanity. Fast forward another seven years and you've got this generation of North American kids.

> Seen it. Heard it. Done it. Bought the T-shirt.

There's no point in pretending it isn't true. There's also no point in blaming the media—the computers and phone lines and video players. The challenge, and the opportunity, is *content*. And when it comes to choosing content, most kids are as unsophisticated as a two-year-old, toddling about, putting everything in his mouth. He doesn't yet know that just because it fits doesn't mean it belongs there.

And don't blame the kids. Children don't create much content. I don't know any *child* pornographers, any grade-school drug lords. Kids consume what adults generate.

Given our culture's content on the subject of profit, I expect adults will continue to sell what people will buy and, given our content on self-gratification, I expect people will continue to buy what's available, and it's an ugly circular argument.

Our society, at the present time, is so caught up by the admiration of success that anything people get away with is admired. We're a sick society in that respect.
— *George Soros* [1]

Our job as adults is to train kids to make sophisticated choices about content.

Like, for instance, sex.

As to the details of sex, our children are sadly sophisticated. As to the mature intimacy of committed sex, our children are *ignorami*.

One of the great misdirections of our age is the notion that sexual sophistication equals maturity. If only it were that easy. Unfortunately, as songwriter Charlie Peacock sadly notes, our boys and girls are making choices better left to men and women. And they pay a heavy price.

Just as they never knew a world without wonderful high-tech goodies, they also never knew a world without high-risk sex, dangerous blood, chlamydia, pelvic inflammatory disease, human papillomavirus (HPV), and AIDS.

- One of every five Americans over the age of eleven has genital herpes.
- About eighty-five percent of women and forty percent of men infected with chlamydia don't know it—yet. Chlamydia is a leading cause of infertility.
- The Centers for Disease Control estimates that 900,000 Americans are infected with HIV, and the majority don't know it.
- Just thirty percent of women who get pregnant before they turn eighteen earn a high school diploma by the time they're thirty.
- Some seventy percent of teenage pregnancies are fathered by men older than twenty.
- Non-marital pregnancy is the number one reason teenage girls go to the hospital.
- Several of the most common STDs are passed by skin-to-skin contact—HIV is among the few that require a break in the skin to gain a new host.
- About a third of adult infertility is caused by STDs.
- American kids are infected with STDs at the rate of about eight thousand a day.
- Between two and four percent of condoms slip or break during use.
- Nearly fifteen percent of people using condoms for contraception get pregnant the first year.
- Condoms are virtually useless against HPV, the most common STD and the most common cause of cervical cancer.[2]

Just thought you oughta know.

Of course, knowing the risk doesn't necessarily

[1] Quoted in *Rolling Stone*, 12.98-1.99, p. 37.
[2] Medical Institute for Sexual Health, P.O. Box 162306, San Antonio, TX, 78716.

keep people from engaging in high-risk behavior. But it could help. Pregnancy rates dipped slightly in the 1990s as kids started waking up to the realities of early sexual activity. And their awareness didn't include some of the data cited here because it was withheld from them until recently.

> Whoa! Withheld? Why on God's earth would anybody keep this kind of information from sexually awake adolescents? I hate to think about it. The worst-case answer has something to do with contempt or distrust or some kind of free-sex fundamentalism that won't let people in on information that isn't *orthodox*. I can only imagine the best-case answer: We don't want to ruin sex for them? We don't want to burden them? That's just plain dumb.

If kids are as smart as they think they are (I think they're that smart, too, by the way), a lot of them will respond to the facts, no matter how inconvenient they are. Those who don't, like those who took up smoking after the disclosure of the tobacco companies' crimes and misdemeanors, are pressing another agenda that has little to do with brain power and just about everything to do with wishing to be taken seriously. They're not wrong to want that.

⸎

It's not all bleak. There's a story about someone asking Ernest Hemingway what makes a good writer. Hemingway replied that a good writer must have a built-in crap detector.

> See, that's the thing. I see lots of kids with highly developed crap detectors. These kids *really* believe nothing they hear and only half of what they see. Which is probably good, because, like it or not, the horse is outta the barn; I don't think we can protect them.

More kids than ever seem to have learned the lessons of family dysfunction: Don't talk, don't trust, don't feel. Consequently, there aren't very many pushovers out there. That's not to say kids are foolproof. But they're wary. Just because an adult or institution says something doesn't mean kids believe it. Give them the information, and they'll decide for themselves. This, too, they learned from us. But they outperform us and far surpass their grandparents in this skill. That being the case, if they're motivated and informed, I wouldn't worry too much about them.

There are those who say we have to worry about kids because we have to take back our culture; lock down the Internet, stop the presses. I can't criticize their zeal. It's just that, in my own childhood, there was never a time when I couldn't find books and magazines to satisfy my interest in sex or bomb-making or anything else. I'm as irritated as I can be about the sex sites that are pushed at me via e-mail. At this moment in life, I don't have an appetite to click on those sites. But that question has always been there: *Do you wanna look at a dirty picture? Do you wanna know how to make a bomb?* If I did, I could. The same is true today; the Internet is just one more delivery platform.

I do have one modest proposal. I live in the middle of the country where prime time television begins at 7:00 P.M. It troubles me that millions of children are wide awake and watching when the more mature programming begins at 8:00. I think that timing gives children just a touch too much access to material that strikes me as inappropriate for younger viewers. The thing is, the same shows are delayed on the West Coast to ensure the largest possible audience for commercial sponsors. Maybe I'm missing something, but aren't we wasting perfectly good commercial air time in the Midwest and Mountain states? I mean, Chicago, Minneapolis/St. Paul, Dallas/Ft. Worth, St. Louis, Kansas City, Denver, Salt Lake City? These are not small markets. Am I the only one who thinks this is a missed opportunity?

[3] One version of Germaine appears in video form in Short Cuts, available from Youth Specialties, 619/440-2333, www.youthspecia lties.com A slightly different version for public performance appears in *Dramatic Pauses* (Grand Rapids: Youth Specialties/ Zondervan, 1995), pp. 17-24.

So, if kids are sophisticated innocents, then . . .

Most kids are equal parts sophisticate and innocent—except when they're not. Sometimes they seem completely, achingly unspoiled. Other times they seem as hard as Nevada hookers. It's awfully confusing. Guess what: It's pretty confusing for them too.

Trying to protect kids from exposure to the world they live in is like trying to put a wetsuit on a porpoise. It's too late; they live in the water. What we *can* do is create the kind of consequential environments that will help kids keep swimming and breathing.

Life without consequences is confounding. Most adults fail to insulate kids from toxic influences. We make it easy for them to engage in high-risk behaviors, then we bail them out so they don't learn from the natural results of their own misdeeds. When kids act out—or just screw up—they don't understand why there's no equal and opposite reaction. In the beginning, the lack of a response may produce elation. They may press the limits further and further in search of the edge. In the long run, they don't feel as though they got away with anything. They're filled with dread. They don't learn the principles of cause and effect until something very big is at stake. They lack an appreciation for the give-and-take of normal social transactions.

I wrote *Germaine* for high school kids to perform and later adapted it to the screen. Believe me, they get it.[3]

Germaine is sixteen, maybe seventeen years old. She's been around the block. If Germaine is the *student body*, it's more because she's available than because she's beautiful. She might even show the struggle with weight that her habits would tend to create. Then again, she might have been on the crystal methamphetamine diet, in which case she would be skinny and have circles under her eyes. Germaine is at the end of her rope. Telling her story is something she never expected to do. She is tired and emotionally flat. Germaine speaks sometimes to her friend, sometimes to the air, sometimes to herself. We hear, but never see, her gentle friend.

[INTERIOR. DUSK. FAST FOOD STORE. The conversation is in progress.]

Germaine: I don't know what to say. I mean I don't know where to start.

Friend: Start at what you think is the beginning. Would that be okay?

Germaine: No. Yes. I guess. I guess I think it started when I was 12—13 maybe. It doesn't matter; it's just that one day I realized guys paid attention to me—older guys.

[EXTERIOR. EVENING. THEATER. We hear **Germaine** voice-over.]

So one night I go to the movies and there's this long line and these guys drive by to see what's playing. And we start talking and stuff and pretty soon I get out of line and into the car. I left my friends there—I still can't believe that.

[EXTERIOR. DUSK. THE STREET. **Germaine** continues.]

Anyway: we drive around and stuff . . . and—and they got me a little drunk, and . . .

Friend: [soothing] It's okay . . .

Germaine: . . . and by the time I got back to the theater my friends were gone. I walked home and made up some lie to my mom . . . and she bought it.

Friend: Why did you lie?

Germaine: I don't know. It was so awful but I felt guilty. I shouldn't have . . . I wish I hadn't done any of it. I wish . . . Oh, man . . . Anyway. Once I lied, I didn't know how to go back. So I didn't. I was . . . well, she bought it so easily . . . I knew I could get away with stuff. So I did. I started meeting guys wherever.

Friend: And . . .

Germaine: And . . . everything. Anything. I don't know. It was like it wasn't even me. I'd let them do stuff and, I don't know, I guess I felt *loved* or *needed* or something. It was weird. It *is* weird.

[INTERIOR. NIGHT. BUS STATION. **Germaine** enters.]

Friend: That's something you didn't have? You didn't feel loved?

Germaine: Yeh, and I thought nobody needed me. I thought it didn't make any difference whether I lived in my house or not; or whether I went to school or not. It was like not being there.

Friend: No difference to . . . ?

Germaine: To anybody. To me. Just a second. [Germaine buys a ticket but we don't know where to, then finds a place to sit down, lights a cigarette.]

Friend: And the boys . . . ?

Germaine: And the boys . . . I had something the boys wanted. I learned to play the game so that, after a while, it was like I had something they *needed*. Do you know what I mean?

Friend: I'm not sure.

Germaine: Yeh, well, I'm not sure either . . .

Friend: Does it seem odd to you that you started *doing* something that was so painful to you? I mean, your introduction to sex was not exactly—I don't know—fairy tale.

Germaine: You got that right.

[We hear an unclear announcement. **Germaine** puts out the cigarette and moves to the departure door.]

[INTERIOR. NIGHT. BUS.]

Germaine: Did you ever hear that song *Sex as a Weapon*? It's like from the early eighties?

Friend: I don't think so.

Germaine: I found it in my mother's tapes. It's about someone who controls people with sex—with love.

Friend: Is that what you were doing?

Germaine: Yeh—well kind've. It was more like *Sex as Money*. You know what I mean? I used sex to buy what I wanted—attention, I guess. And to feel needed . . .

Friend: And did that work for you?

Germaine: In a way, for a while . . . I think I thought that if guys needed me I could have—I don't know—power over them, I guess. But it doesn't feel *right* now—here. It never really felt right. It felt *good*, at least some of the time, but it never really felt right.

Friend: And there's a difference between feeling good and feeling good about yourself . . .

Germaine: Yeh. There's a big difference.

Friend: Which is . . .

Germaine: Which is that, when love—when even sex—is power, it's like it's not love anymore. And that doesn't feel right. That doesn't make me feel good about myself—at all. Am I making sense?

Friend: You're making a lot of sense.

[EXTERIOR. NIGHT. We see the bus pass by. They are quiet for a moment. INTERIOR. NIGHT. BUS. The **Friend** speaks again.]

Friend: Where is God in all this?

Germaine: About a million miles away. I haven't talked to God about anything real for a long time. I've thought about it, but I haven't done it.

Friend: How come?

Germaine: You have to ask? . . . I did talk with God about one thing. . . . I told him I wanted to die.

Friend: And . . .

Germaine: He wouldn't let me.

[EXTERIOR. DAWN. BUS STOP. The bus pulls into the shot and stops.] **Germaine** exits the bus and the bus pulls away.

[Germaine addresses her friend.]

Germaine: You ready?

Friend: Are you?

[**Germaine** shrugs.]

Friend: Why did you decide to tell me this? What do you want to *do* about it?

Germaine: Why am I telling you this . . . I don't know exactly. I know I've carried this alone for too long. I know I'm sick of it. I know I tried to eat and drink and smoke and screw my brains out. And here I am. Nothing could be worse than this. I don't care any more. Having my mom and stepfather find out? Doesn't matter. I tried everything . . . But you're right: It's time to do somethin'. Maybe even . . . I don't know. Somethin'.

[**Germaine** turns and walks toward the rising sun. A train passes, its horn blowing mournfully.]

The only antidote to this kind of poison is an early and appropriately consequential environment. And that can't be bought off-the-shelf; you have to cook it up at home from a family recipe. It requires thought and attention to minding the stove. Of course, that's difficult when there's so much going on. And when isn't there too much going on? If you have more than one child, the pace never slows. You can spend all day playing Mother May I. It's easy to go to extremes—to be too permissive or too controlling—just to keep the pot from boiling over.

> Control says *no* before the question is finished. There's nothing to talk about, really. Everyone understands the rules. There's no room for interpretation because there's no need for interpretation. If a child can't grasp that, he certainly can't be trusted to operate outside the rules, now, can he?

Controlling is neat and clean: It fosters the abuse of alcohol, cocaine, and sedatives. A child who perceives that his parents are too controlling—especially if he thinks the control is hostile—tends toward resistance, aggressiveness, vandalism, acting out sexually, and a bit of hostility of his own.

Permissiveness, on the other hand, knows no limits. For reasons that may or may not be obvious, the permissive adult sets no boundaries.

> To be fair, it's hard to find an adult who'll admit she doesn't set boundaries. "I set boundaries," she'll say. "The kids just ignore them." Reminds me of the "No Trespassing" signs where we used to hunt when I was a boy. The signs were posted on barbed-wire fences, which we figured were there to keep cattle in, not to keep us out. So we climbed a lot of those fences. But not all. We learned which signs were for real by the consequences attached to being on the wrong side of the fence.

Children who perceive that their parents are too permissive feel out of control in a way different from those who believe their parents are too strict. The child of permissiveness is likely to be manipulative, disrespectful, unmotivated, excessive, and unable to draw boundaries between herself and others. If she uses drugs, she's likely to choose marijuana. If she thinks her parent is hostile she may gravitate to hallucinogens and inhalants.[4]

[4] These predictors are based on the findings of Fred Streit, Donald Halsted, and J. Pietro Pascale, published in the *International Journal of Addictions*, volume nine, number five (1974), pp. 749-755, and summarized by H. Stephen Glenn and Jane Nelsen in *Raising Self-Reliant Children in a Self-Indulgent World* (Rocklin, CA: Prima Publishing/St. Martins Press, 1989) pp. 208-216.

If we put permissiveness and control at two ends of a continuum, the ideal lies in the middle.

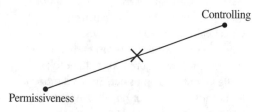

All things being equal, children who perceive their parents to be neither permissive nor controlling feel they have a fighting chance at life. They believe they'll be heard fairly in any circumstance, be it a request or a dispute. Therefore, manipulation makes no sense and there's no cause for resistance. If the parent seems unusually controlling on some matter, the child is more likely to seek dialog to understand why this normally reasonable adult seems unreasonable at this point. If the parent seems overly permissive, the child may initiate a dialog to ensure she has understood the agreement and may even offer additional information to help the adult make a more informed decision.

Seriously. Applied consistently over a child's life, this stuff works. There will be tests, no doubt about it. But, overall, it's a win/win and, unless something else is seriously out of whack, everyone can see that.

Balancing permissiveness and control can even be retrofitted in an adult-child relationship. But not overnight. If you have a history of controlling and you begin now to listen before you decide, I promise your kid will test you. By the same token, if you've never drawn a single line in the sand and you start requiring more reasonable standards of conduct, your child will squawk so loud the neighbors will think you're channeling Joe Stalin in the Great Purge.

Here's a strategy:

Begin by acknowledging past failure. Something like this may be appropriate: "I've been doing a lot of thinking lately and I have to admit I've been, frankly, too strict about some things." If permissiveness is your poison, try something like "Yadda, yadda . . . I have to admit I haven't given you very clear guidelines about some things." The two tracks converge here: "First, I want to say I'm sorry. That wasn't fair to you. I hope you'll forgive me for not thinking more clearly about this in the past. The other thing I want you to know is that I'm going to try to do a better job in the future. I'm going to try to listen more carefully and make decisions that make better sense. Okay?"

That's enough. If your child wants to know more about what you mean, tell him. But don't let it turn into an argument. This is your press conference: Make your announcement, answer a couple of questions, and excuse yourself to take care of urgent national security matters. Or not. If things are going well, move right into the next step.

Discuss the new plan. Begin with something like, "When you need something from me, please time your request so it's convenient for both of us to give the conversation our full attention. I'll try to do the same when I need something from you." Emphasize your promise to listen carefully and ask for more information if you don't understand. Ask for the same consideration. Acknowledge that sometimes things come up suddenly: "When that happens, I'll try to give you the best decision I can under the circumstances. Does that seem fair?" Keep talking about it until it seems fair.

Create a safety net. "I told you I'm going to try to do a better job of listening to you. And I am. But I have to admit I've got some old habits that may be hard to break. Could we come up with a signal for when you don't feel listened to? I don't mean throwing things. Let's come up with something either of us can say when we don't feel listened to. When you give me the signal, I agree to stop and ask you to help me understand what you're feeling or what you mean—and you can do the same for me, okay?"

If necessary, outlast them. Do what you said you'd do. Listen carefully. Ask for more information, including emotional information. "This seems pretty important to you. Tell me about that." If your child doesn't feel listened to, be responsive when he tells you so. If you don't feel listened to, use the signal you agreed to. (*Don't,* under any circumstances, use the signal to manipulate your child. She'll figure it out and she won't trust you for a long, long time.) Negotiate a plan together and set out to make it happen in good faith.

If things go according to plan, congratulations all around! If they don't—and I can just about promise they won't in the beginning—go to the Training Tips on pages 127-128 to find out why. There's about a twenty-five percent chance you're the one who screwed it up.

> Don't get all cocky. The chance it's your kid's fault and not yours isn't seventy-five percent— it's about the same: twenty-five percent. There's about a fifty percent chance you *both* got it wrong. But don't get all down in the mouth. You're still learning to do this, right?

If the deal falls apart, acknowledge it, set up a new plan, and try it again. And again. For as long as it takes.

I wouldn't recommend assigning stern consequences on the first agreement. That telegraphs that you anticipate failure. The consequences for not getting it right in the beginning are that you revisit the agreement and start again. Try to initiate a first agreement with a low impact should things go awry. Ease into more significant consequences as necessary. If your kid buys into the new deal, you may never have to set specific consequences for failure. But if you believe you're being taken to the cleaners, by all means set reasonable, appropriate consequences in advance.

FOR MORE ON NEGOTIATING, GO TO PAGE 121 AND 170.

There are two classes of consequences: Natural and Logical.

Natural consequences flow directly out of the circumstances in a cause-and-effect relationship. Natural consequences are beautiful because you don't have to think them up; they just *are*. Let's say you have an agreement about managing money and your child blows his wad on some impulsive purchase. Then he comes to you to bail him out when he wants to go to a concert or buy a warm-up jacket. The natural consequence of his spending—this is especially important if he's a habitual offender—is that he doesn't go to the concert or he doesn't get the jacket. However difficult, this is small potatoes compared to not having a down payment or not being able to pay his taxes in a few years because he spent all the money.

> You and I can have a cappuccino and talk about how the ante will go up in the future because we know what that looks like. But if, in the heat of the moment, you try to talk with your kid about higher stakes in "the real world," it'll come off like moralizing. Let it be. He's smart, just inexperienced. That's what this is about. He'll get it. You can process it later to make sure.

Logical consequences are not so beautiful. Apart from missing a meal or losing some sleep, there's no *natural* consequence to coming home late. So, if necessary, you must create a *logical* consequence. You may find it helpful to invite the habitual offender to join you in the invention of logical consequences. Some possibilities for coming home late:

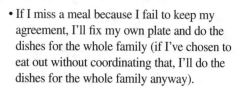

- If I miss a meal because I fail to keep my agreement, I'll fix my own plate and do the dishes for the whole family (if I've chosen to eat out without coordinating that, I'll do the dishes for the whole family anyway).
- If I fail to return on time, I'll move my curfew up an hour tomorrow to ensure the extra time necessary to get home (and pay another consequence if I miss the new curfew).

Other examples:

- If I bring the car home with less than a quarter of a tank of gas, I'll wash it within 48 hours.
- If I can't keep my clothes reasonably well-sorted and off the floor, I'll do my own laundry. If I can't do my own laundry to a mutually agreed-upon standard, I'll pay to have it done. If I can't afford to pay to have my laundry done, I'll figure a way to keep my clothes reasonably well-sorted and off the floor.
- If I can't manage my time in such a way as to get my homework done and get adequate rest, nutrition, and exercise and still have some fun, *and* still be a participating member of this family, I'll get help from the expert of my choice. If I still can't manage, I'll get help from (Yikes!) you.

Create your own list. Susan and I chose not to care too much about the tidiness of Kate's room. Come to think of it, Susan shows considerable tolerance for the state of my home office. That's what doors are for. But Kate (and I) always showed great respect for the common areas of our home. To steal an idea from Disneyland, at our house bedrooms and offices are "backstage" and not part of the tour. But what's on the tour is kept guest-ready at all times.

⁓

Of course there are more serious stakes when it comes to matters of health, safety, and sexuality. I hope you don't have to begin with building a consequential environment in those areas. If you do, the principles are the same. It's just not as easy to talk about. Set up a new plan and try it again. And again.

> I'm the adult. If he resists, everything about my life has prepared me to outlast my kid on this. I know if it takes a year to get it in place, that's a small investment of time and energy for something that will serve both of us for the rest of our lives.

Everything about this strategy is meant to express respect for you and your child. This is not about one of you winning at the expense of the other.

⁓

There's another continuum in nurturing kids. It's the line between heavy involvement on one extreme and unbridled freedom on the other. Parents who aren't heavily involved with their infants are in for a world of pain. It's no secret

that bonding requires intense contact. The greater the contact, the stronger the bond. But the same level of involvement with a child of three is unhealthy. At the age of six, it's smothering. At the age of twelve, it's crippling. At the age of sixteen, it's a Tennessee Williams play—some would call it emotional incest.

There are exceptions where heavy involvement may not do the trick. Relatively new psychiatric diagnoses center around attachment disorders, the inability or failure to bond with parents and, subsequently, with others. Unattached people behave in ways that span the gap between creepy and dangerous. Violence, sadism, sexual predation, and animal torture may, any or all of them, be present in unattached people. In an odd twist of traits, unattached people may be quite engaging, even charming. But loyalty is out of the question. Depending on the source, unattached people are immoral or amoral. Whichever, they seem baffled by appeals to morality or ethics. They may be persuaded, more or less, to conform to social norms in order to stay out of trouble, but "right" and "wrong" don't make much sense to them. I know and even love people with attachment disorders. Is it mental illness or intensely self-absorbed evil? I'm not sure it's that simple. The likelihood that you're involved with an unattached child is very small. If you think you may be, consult your doctor. She can help you find the information you need.—jb

Kids require increasing levels of freedom. Otherwise, they either become inappropriately dependent or they run away as fast as they can. Too much freedom too soon is dangerous. Appropriate freedom withheld too long can be debilitating. What's called for is balance. So let's add a positive and a negative to our continuum. Permissiveness is negative, but Freedom is positive. Controlling is negative, Involvement is positive.

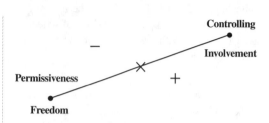

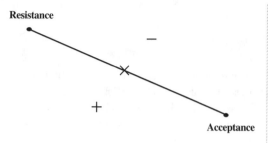

If things go well, by the time our children reach adolescence we can be hands-off about lots of things—but never disengaged. Permissiveness—about money, curfew, diet, exercise, friends—is never a good thing. Freedom, on the other hand, is inevitable. Eventually, your child will be on her own. Unless, of course, you plan to keep her under your control for the rest of your life. I say *your* life because she's likely to survive you and live on as an emotional and relational cripple. Some day she'll wake up to answer the questions: "Why am I hobbling around at my age? What happened?" And, after a great deal of thought, her answer will be, "Ah, I remember now: My mother bound my feet when I was a child. I suppose she hoped it would make me attractive." Nobody wants that.

But that's not to say you can't stay involved in age-appropriate ways for the rest of your child's life. I say your *child's* life because if you balance freedom with involvement, you'll become a genuine friend to your adult child and he'll never forget you.

Another continuum in parenting is the tension between Acceptance and Resistance.

Kids can and will take a lot of disappointment from adults if they're convinced the adults accept them. This is the cornerstone of abusive relationships. For a long time, maybe into adulthood, the child believes his parent's protestations of love and endures verbal, physical, even sexual assault. Crazy? You bet. But completely understandable. Love is not blind; love is stupid. This kind of love is utterly well-intentioned and sadly stupid.

On the other extreme, kids who believe their parents *reject* them tend to be wary and distrustful despite evidence to the contrary. However mistaken he may be, a boy who thinks his father holds him in contempt is likely to turn into a young man with the same opinion.

You may not think there's a balance between acceptance and resistance. We've come to believe that acceptance must be unconditional and absolute and, in a way, we've come to believe the right thing. If by unconditional love you mean, *Of course I want to love my child with my whole heart, no matter how she may succeed or fail,* then sign me up.

The problem comes when acceptance takes a permissive turn. If by unconditional love you mean,

I will accept anything my child does or says no matter how destructive it may be, I'll have to pass. There are behaviors I must resist even while my child remains wholly accepted by me.

I speak theoretically here because my daughter has engaged in none of those behaviors. But my father did.

On his infrequent visits to our home, my father used to ogle my wife and daughter, used to sneak up on them and walk in on them when they were dressing. He never touched either of them inappropriately, but he certainly put them in awkward situations. Minimize it if you wish, but no woman should suffer that indignity.

I'm sad to admit that I didn't create enough emotional safety in my family to find out what my father did until after his death. So I never did anything to stop it. I'm *happy* to report that, in the last year of his life, my dad and I came clean with each other about a great many things, including our sexual compulsions. He couldn't bring himself to mention this one. Maybe, in his mind, it was so minor compared to other things he admitted that it hardly registered on the screen. Maybe he was just too ashamed to say it. It certainly registered with Susan and Kate and, after his death, with me. And had I known about it when he was doing it, I'd like to think I would've done something about it.

Some time later I did resist unacceptable behavior from my mother. She is a wonderfully gentle person today but was not always so. She came for a visit at a particularly fragile time in our family life. I took special care to explain our circumstances to her, asking her to please, please, please, cut us some extra slack. I felt the need to outline our situation carefully because I had a history of misunderstanding, and sometimes harsh disagreement, with my mom. I didn't want to make any assumptions in this case. My family was strung very tight, grieving like crazy, under financial pressure, feeling pretty lost. Mom listened sympathetically and agreed to be especially tender.

Less than twenty-four hours later she exploded with a fury that put Susan and me in a tailspin. And it was about something I thought merited no more than a polite disagreement—the business strategy of a mutual acquaintance. I'm pretty sure I was sarcastic about the choice our friend made. But I was completely unprepared for the intensity and personal nature of my mother's response.

We all went to our rooms. When Kate came home from school, she found what seemed to be an empty house. Kate and Susan left and I knocked on the guest room door. Sad but resolute, I told my mom she'd better cut short her visit with us. I reminded her of the conversation we had the day before. I told her what I thought was necessary to make our home safe again. There was no rage from either of us. It was quiet, direct, and very painful. And it was loving, even though I chose to not accept her behavior.

My firmness in that event was the catalyst for a new beginning in our relationship. We developed a respectful, dignified, loving connection. She never seemed to grasp the weight her angry words carried over the first twenty years of my marriage and, eventually, I told her I would stop trying to explain it further unless she initiated the conversation. We talked about it once or twice after that, without resolving anything. My wife still doesn't feel safe with my mother, and it's been a long time since they've seen each other. I feel sad about that. But it's not about any lack of love, and it's not over until it's over.

When you put this all together, you get this matrix:

Resistance

Controlling

Involvement

Permissiveness

Freedom

Acceptance

The axes balance controlling with permissiveness, involvement with freedom, and acceptance with resistance.

The negative side of the matrix, including permissiveness, resistance, and controlling, is the badlands. No child should grow up there. At the risk of redundancy, I'm not in favor of resisting children as people. Perhaps I should boldly change the other end of this continuum to read *unconditional acceptance* but I've already altered the language used in the research. Instead of Acceptance versus Resistance, the research used the language of *love* versus *hostility*. Heaven knows both exist in many families. Maybe I'm just squeamish. [Note to self: Work this out. Get help if necessary.]

I'm much more comfortable with the positive side of the matrix, including involvement, accept-ance, and freedom. But, if I'm honest, I have to admit that what I long for is not merely involvement, acceptance, and freedom. What I really want—and I believe I get it from my wife and daughter, a few close friends, and the God who made me—is love that calls out and improves the very best in me and resists the worst in me. It's love that keeps me on the hook no matter how badly I think I want off.

The love I long for, I long to give the people I love.

What's the most significant thing you read or thought about in this chapter?

Why do you think that's so significant?

What do you think you might want to do about that?

Don't take my word for it. What did you read here that's worth checking with a kid?

Demotivated

3.2

Modern kids don't play by the rules. They have no loyalty to traditional political parties or religious structures. They tend to vote unpredictably, if they vote at all.

Waiting

I'm not just sitting here. Doing nothing.
I'm waiting. Waiting for something worth doing.
I'm not self-absorbed. I'm introspective.
> I'm paying attention. I'm watching.
> Listening. Waiting for something meaningful.

I'm not lazy and I'm not unmotivated.
> Demotivated, maybe. Underchallenged,
> certainly. Sorry, but I'm just underwhelmed
> by shallow dreams. Unimpressed by mean-
> ingless ambition, colorless relationships,
> broken promises.

Slacker?! Yeh, right.
Show me one ideal worth dying for. Let me
> glimpse one thing worth living for. Do that
> and the wait is over. Ask me a big enough
> question and I'll answer with my life.

Waiting is the text of a short film I wrote for a gathering of twenty-somethings. The organizers wanted a motivational piece—something to kick-start the last hours of a daylong conference on change.

The movie was well received by the young crowd and the program people. Not so much by the Boomers who paid for it. In fact, the Deep Pockets were disenchanted with the whole gathering. This is just my opinion—I could be wrong—but I think they were hoping for a means of co-opting the twenty-somethings into their vision for America's future.

I'm sure you recall *co-optation* from first-year sociology. Or were you one of those *serious* students, too focused on *real* academics to bother with sociology? (Oops. Did I say that out loud? Did that sound angry at all?) Co-optation is the practice of recruiting potentially troublesome, usually non-formal, leaders into management positions before they incite the workaday employees to discontent over low pay or dangerous working conditions. It's based on one of the oldest of American business principles: If you can't beat 'em, buy 'em.

Those darned kids at this conference! It didn't take more than a few hours to see they weren't interested in being co-opted. The conference was supposed to be the pilot for a nationwide series of events. Didn't happen. After a day of watching and listening to the concerns of these young folk, the organizers scrubbed the mission. I wish I could say this is the only time I've seen that kind of thing.

My work includes helping organizations think about how their mission will survive after they're gone. What's disconcerting is how often someone voices the question that's apparently on the minds of many: "Is there any way to skip this generation and still survive?"

The answer is, "No. Why do you ask?"

I know why they ask. Modern kids don't play by the rules. They have no loyalty to traditional political parties or religious structures. They tend to vote unpredictably, if they vote at all. They tend to make up their own religious dogma rather than accept something warmed-over.

> College is no longer the goal. The dirty little secret my peers and I can't tell is that a B.A. is no longer the Golden Ticket, it's preparation for temp work or grad school, or both. —Brian

> Work is not enjoyable. —Eli

Career? Kids can hardly even face the prospect of a *job. American Demographics* columnist Marc Spiegler thinks he understands: "What seems like apathetic hedonism actually represents a fairly informed bet," he says. "Why put up with the cubicled world's woes when its promised delayed gratification is an ever more dicey proposition?"[1]

Anti-sabbatical: A job taken with the sole intention of staying only for a limited period of time (often one year). The intention is usually to raise enough funds to partake in another, more personally meaningful activity such as watercolor sketching in Crete or designing computer knit sweaters in Hong Kong. Employers are rarely informed of intentions.

—Douglas Coupland [2]

Suppose you grew up eating dinners you prepared, alone in front of the television, because the adults in your life weren't actually in your life, they were at work. Suppose your folks can't remember where they were when the Challenger blew up in 1984, but remember everything about the day the stock market blew up in 1987—and now benchmark every pain to the pain they felt that day. Suppose you watched your dad bust his hump sixty or eighty hours a week for a company that downsized him because it was good for quarterly earnings. If those things were true of your childhood, how would you feel about joining the rat race? Real excited, I bet.

To many of us, the ambivalence of the young looks like a lack of commitment. They are slow to give their loyalty; we take it for untrustworthiness. They fidget when some vice president starts repeating herself in a meeting; we think they're unfocused. They multi-task; we think they're slacking off.

Our young folks are pretty much worn out with self-fulfilling prophecies.

> We don't expect much from you, just try not to cause too much trouble, okay? We're trying to figure out how to get you into the asset column but, frankly, at this point you're a liability. Which is not to say we don't appreciate your disposable income. We are not ungrateful and if, from time to time, we fail to express our appreciation, it's only because we're caught up in devising new, better ways to get your money. So, for now, just leave it on the counter and please don't let the door hit you on your way out.

I Buy, Therefore I Am? It's a message that paralyzes lots of young Americans: "Is that all you think I'm good for? Well that sucks."

Alfred Adler suggested that children see themselves reflected in the eyes of their parents. What they see there is *get in line, stay in line, color inside the lines*. The young have a lamentable capacity to live down to the expectations of their elders.

[1] Quoted in *Time*, June 9, 1997, p. 60.
[2] Douglas Coupland, *Generation X* (New York: St. Martin's Press, 1991), p. 35.

> Lazy, disaffected, drug doin', MTV watchin', video game playin' snots? Okay, we can do that.—Brian
>
> If you get burned enough times you learn not to put your hand on the stove.—Kate

So, they just check out. At least that's how it looks to the people who monitor America's values most closely: advertising agencies. America's marketers say young people are a moving target, unpredictable, hard to reach. Look how the pop music industry had to diversify to reach much smaller clusters of listeners than in the past. It's not that there are fewer buyers; it's that the marketplace is splintered into two dozen mutating genres, none of them likely to be the Next Big Thing on the scale of Elvis, the Beatles, Fleetwood Mac, or Michael Jackson. I'm not making qualitative observations here, I'm just thinking about sales. (Michael Jackson's *Thriller* sold more than 40 million copies worldwide; the best-selling album of 1998, the soundtrack from *Titanic*, sold less than a quarter of that number.) Who knows, it could all change tomorrow. But nobody in the music business is counting on it.

These days, *Big* is not all that big on television either. Traditional broadcast networks have acquired cable operations—and their content—like a tobacco company snapping up snack food manufacturers. With an important difference: The tobacco company was trying to look legitimate, the networks need viewers, and they need them right now.

Have you watched the *X Games* on television? The nineties were nearly over before we had the chance, and then only on the offbeat ESPN2 sports cable channel. Then ABC bought ESPN and we got to watch at least part of the *X Games* on channel seven instead of channel ninety-nine. Two things were apparent immediately:

First, *X Games* competitors are world-class athletes (they just don't happen to throw balls or hit people like *real* athletes).

Second, by the time the rest of us tuned in, the *X Games* had already captured and mobilized a core audience of twelve- to thirty-four-year-old male consumers who had been written off as too difficult to reach (difficult meaning they don't care about what we already know how to do). The first year the games were televised on ABC, Adidas, AT&T, Chevrolet, and the U.S. Marines climbed aboard like refugees. And why not? It's where the money is going to be. Only one in five American kids played football, softball, baseball, or volleyball as a team sport in 1994.[3]

The backbone of extreme sports appears at first to be nontraditional, individual events. I don't think that's quite right. Take half-pipe skating for example. Half-pipe skaters perform skateboard tricks in half cylinders constructed of plywood. Gravity drags skaters from the rim of the half pipe to the floor of the trough, and inertia pulls them up the other side. Beyond the physics is pure, graceful, athletic skill in the best skaters. The rest wear out a bunch of kneepads and have dings on their helmets.

In the wild, half-pipe skating is extraordi-

[3] U.S. Census Bureau, Statistical Abstract of the United States, 1994, table 406.

narily social. It began with groups of adolescent boys and young men doing skateboard tricks in storm drains and flood-control culverts—each taking his turn in the pipe while the others watched. Some wag suggested the name comes from the likelihood that inhaling about half a pipe of exotic herbs precedes hair-raising stunts like 540-degree board-over-head spins four feet above the pipe rim and about twenty feet above the floor. These guys are real jocks. They just don't happen to care much about All-American team sports. They didn't play baseball or pee-wee football. They skated. They didn't work with coaches, they worked with their friends and, over time, the people they skated with became rivals as well as friends. Skaters are more like surfers than ballplayers. Different skill set, different schedule, same drive to excel outside the norm.

The surfing metaphor leads us to another group of high-achieving young people who are hard for their parents to figure out. In addition to extreme jocks, we've raised a baffling generation of digital kids. They learn off the screen better than most of us. They follow obscure links from topic to topic better than most of us. They multi-task, moving between computer screen and hard copy, with music playing, while using the phone for a conference call with their study group. When they were younger, they got in trouble with 900 and 976 numbers, just trying to see what all the fuss was about. No one was happier to see the advent of flat-rate online services; now they're online for hours (though many have so little sense of time, they don't know how long).

They know dirty tricks like e-mail bombing, so don't get them riled. If they haven't done it themselves, they know someone who's hacked into a system where he didn't belong. They're bored at school—too linear, too slow. They're like Bill Gates, except they hate Bill Gates, not because he sold out, but for trying to gain a monopoly with software they think is crap. Get used to them. In many ways, they're our future—the geeks who inherit the earth.

We would be remiss if we failed to acknowledge the *Stars*—the good sons and Daddy's girls so obsessed with approval they're sitting ducks for eating disorders, suckers for short cuts, cheating, deception, false perfectionism, and dropping out. They are approval junkies, willing to do anything to get the nod from . . . someone. They look for approval at home first, but if they can't get it from the ones they love, they learn to love the ones from whom they get it. They're fish in a barrel for predatory adults and older adolescents who don't even have to bait a hook; just drop it in and see what bites.

> I feel sorry for these kids because they're willing to play by our rules. They try so hard to make it work. They're so naïve, they don't see the bait and switch. We told them sex was everything. Okay, then, they did sex to death. They're just fifteen years old and they can't imagine why sex is such a big deal. Sex is just another social skill, like making small talk. They're sick of it; who needs it?

There's more.

We told them you are what you own. They bought it.

We told them pain is bad. They did everything they could to avoid pain, or to kill it. Now they have just the tiniest of dependent relationships with a drug called _____.

Fill in the blank with whatever fits, you freaking basket case! Oh, does that hurt your feelings? See, there's your problem: You still have feelings. You better do something about that because you know what? Pain is bad and if you feel pain, *you're* bad. Get it?

They get it. And they'll keep trying to banish the pain until they die, or until they nearly die and learn to live instead. Forgive me for bleeding on you; I didn't know I was opening a vein. Yet another piece of unfinished business.

Last on the list, because they are least in our culture, are the poor.

In 1994, a quarter of America's kids were poor in any given month. A third were poor for at least two months. The median length of children's poverty spells in 1993 and 1994 was just over five months. Four percent of children who were not poor in 1993 became poor in 1994. One out of ten was poor throughout 1993 and 1994.[4] A quarter of poor children, nearly 3.5 million, had no health insurance in 1996.[5]

For ten percent of our children, life is relentlessly difficult. For the next twenty percent, by income, the misery comes and goes, and comes again.

Of all the kids accused of laziness, the poor take the hardest hit. The national unemployment rate in the nineties dropped to encouraging lows. But in America's poorest communities the unemployment rate among poor teenagers was up to ten times the national rate.

Why harp on the nineties? They're over!

I don't mean to harp. I'm just saying our children were growing up in the nineties (and the eighties, which were worse) and during those years our poorest children got poorer.

I know we've got our best people working on it night and day. That doesn't matter to the childhoods of those who grew up before we sounded the alarm. Which means those children, now young men and women, may never have worked, may never have had a successful job interview, may never have been socialized in the niceties of shaking hands, making eye contact, saying their names clearly.

Guess what else poor kids don't do. They don't go to college. That means they're less likely to raise their own children with the advantages of Middle America. And the cycle continues. Marginalized in almost every way, barely employable, frightening to Boomers because they just don't look right. Where do they even start?

I know a kid in Chicago who endured the pain of barber college to earn the right to pay $120 a week to rent a chair in a big shop where kids he grew up with routinely buy, sell, and deliver controlled substances for large amounts of money —money they use to buy gold jewelry and cell phones—while he labors to build a clientele and make ends meet on eight-dollar haircuts. Help him, Jesus! He is taking, for his neighborhood and age, the road less traveled.

4 U.S. Census Bureau, Current Population Reports, Household Economic Studies, P70-63, July, 1998.
5 U.S. Census Bureau. Census Brief, CENBR/98-1, March 1998.

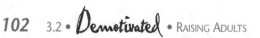

So, if kids are demotivated, then . . .

Because so many of our kids are demotivated by the conviction that adults don't expect anything from them, our course is almost obvious.

We can turn that around so fast it'll make their heads spin. I don't know if you noticed, but all the labor-saving devices we introduced since the fifties resulted in longer work weeks and more household chores than ever. Why, in the name of all that's efficient, would we fail to train and empower younger Americans to help with that work? Just because there are no cows to milk doesn't mean we can't give our children legitimate work to do. Work that keeps us up late or gets us up early. Let the little darlings earn their keep; they'll love you for it.

But we have to give them the right stuff. That thing about not sending a boy to do a man's job still makes sense. We're so obsessed with over-achievement, even Superman is just an average guy. That's nuts.

> Take Science Fairs. We all know Roscoe didn't make that cold fusion converter. In fact, by your red-rimmed eyes, we can tell you stayed up all night working on it yourself. Or you have a nasty case of pink-eye. Why? So everyone who knows you're Roscoe's mom will be proud of you? To launch his career in the hard sciences? Who are we kidding?

Give kids something meaningful to do. Over-achieving is generally meaningless. It's more about appearance than function. Our children need meaningful work. I mean they really *need* it. And it's not that hard to find. It's right in our own homes and requires a minimal investment of brain capital to develop. If you're not sure where to begin, try Square One.

Square One: Stop giving allowances. Really. I mean, what's that about? Does someone give you an allowance just for showing up on the planet? There are things your child needs, and I wouldn't recommend doling out French fries or undergarments one at a time. But why confuse needs with wants? Why mix your obligation to look after your child's needs with an obligation to give away discretionary income? Once the needs are met, assuming you can manage that and assuming you can agree on a working definition of "need," give your child an economic education by letting her create value in exchange for cash. Start simple and work up.

When Kate approached high school, we struck a deal. She would work summer jobs, but during the school year her job was to work on a whopping financial aid package for college. In exchange we agreed to provide her with x dollars each month to spend at her discretion. Anything she earned during the summer became part of her stake. When she started driving, we invested in an old toaster which we gassed, maintained, then sold the day after she went to college. Did I mention Kate went to the private college of her choice with a financial aid package so good we couldn't have sent her to a state school for less?

Kate's capacity to make that her job during high school was predicated on a lifetime of contributing to our family. We didn't pay her for doing the dishes. That's a family job everybody has to do. But we did create opportunities for enterprise, like the time she transferred the contents of my paper Rolodex into an electronic address book. And we tied the regular dollars we gave her each month to

FOR MORE ON TRAINING, GO TO PAGE 127.

the value of her participation with us in making the household work smoothly. That included washing dishes, picking up after the dog, vacuuming, cooking—things we all do to make our life together work (okay, I don't cook, I warm, but you get the point). Along the way, Kate learned to budget her money because there wasn't an unlimited pool. That's Economic Education 101: Work creates income, which spends easier than it accumulates.

Think about it. Make an inventory, then strike a new deal or reposition your existing arrangement. You can make this happen.

Communicate appropriate expectations. Inspiration turns expectations to motivation.

> Hey! You're startin' to sound like one of those motivational speakers: Motivation, Inspiration, Perspiration. Make your point.

Create an environment where expectations for outcomes and processes are clear, and kids have a fighting chance at success, which is very inspirational. Said plain: Success inspires kids and inspired kids get things done.

I'm on record in favor of *learning* more than bringing home good grades. I think learning is a pretty good predictor of decent grades; I'm less sold on grades as a predictor of learning. Communicating that core expectation, and reinforcing it over time, created a clear motivation for Kate. She put in the hard work necessary to learn, and the grades took care of themselves.

When Kate got her driver's license, we had a brief conversation about accidents. "You're going to have an accident," I told her. "Sooner or later, it will happen because, no matter how hard you try,

accidents happen. That's why we have a word to describe that category of experience: 'It was an accident.'" She looked at me with mild surprise. I say strange things from time to time; she was waiting for the punch line. Here it is, or was: "What we're asking is that you do everything in your power to ensure that your accident is minor. Does that seem fair?" She thought it seemed fair enough, and set about driving with such care that the tiny dent in the rear fender of the family car is a gentle reminder that, even when we're careful, accidents happen. That's the only mishap she's had in half a dozen years of driving. It probably won't be her last. But the next one will be on her insurance, which probably won't matter because it, too, will most likely be minor. That's the value of a clear expectation about an outcome (relative safety) and a process (careful driving). She understood it, she embraced it, she performed superbly.

Provide appropriate training. Nobody knows anything they didn't learn. Teach your children well. Correct instead of criticizing. Train them as you would like to be trained.

Enough said.

🦎 What's the most significant thing you read or thought about in this chapter?

🦎 Why do you think that's so significant?

🦎 What do you think you might want to do about that?

🦎 Don't take my word for it. What did you read here that's worth checking with a kid?

Alone, Afraid, Unsafe

3.3

Once upon a time,

I assumed the world

was relatively safe.

Yes, there was

The Bomb, but

that was about it.

I'm Not

It blows a little harder now and I pick up
    my pace
the cool breeze turns warmer
I roll in the air and think what an easy life I have
The wind stops
I fall onto a hot, black, and scary soil
the rumble begins
it trembles the earth
I hear a loud grumble in the upper depths of
    the ground
the yellow monster appears
he doesn't notice me
I am shattered into millions of petite sticks
just sticks
I lay on the road and ask another tumbleweed
    whizzing by
why this had to happen
he goes on and does not answer and I think to
    myself . . . was my life worth it
I still say . . . was I worth being on the earth or
    just another tumbleweed in the wind
maybe I wasn't and worse yet because I am still
    breathing maybe
I ' M   N O T ! !
make something of your life

—BEN (on waiting for the bus
to take him to school)

Once upon a time, I assumed the world was rela-tively safe. Yes, there was The Bomb, but that was about it.

I thought I knew every kid in my school whose parents were divorced. Looking back, I doubt that. But I grew up with an assumption about parents being married.

I grew up with a lot of assumptions about the durability of relationships, the relative safety of the streets where I played, our social mores around honesty and sex and citizenship.

A lot of my assumptions were vapor; I know that now. Still, I grew up in a place where people acted as if those assumptions were valid even if they weren't true to life.

My daughter grew up in a very different time, in a generation dogged by violence of every kind—or neglected, left to their own devices. They tend to think of themselves as survivors.

> Do you want to put this list in order of common-ness? I would rank divorce first, neglect and substance abuse tied for second, and abortion/abuse/violence third. That's only from my personal experience though.—Alice

Survivors of Divorce. The issues surround-ing the children of divorce and remarriage are the stuff of legend. And there are a lot of those children. About 870,000 American kids were involved in divorce in 1970—something more than a million kids every year since 1975. In 1995, more than seven million kids under the age of eighteen lived with a divorced single parent. Tough all around.

Survivors of Neglect. The term "latchkey kids" was coined to describe people now in their twenties and thirties. In one way or another, most young men and women feel relationally dispossessed.

Survivors of Substance Abuse. Every young American knows someone who was injured or killed by the abuse of alcohol or other drugs. Just ask around.

Survivors of Abortion. One of every four U.S. pregnancies between 1976 and 1992 was terminated by induced abortion.[1] Some young Americans think of abortion as their Vietnam.

Survivors of Violent Crime. To many young folk, drive-by shootings are what The Bomb was to us—a constant, dull, unsettling apprehension, *this could be the day*.

Survivors of Sexual Abuse. It's a given: Molestation, date rape, and sexual intimidation are jagged social debris through which young women pick their way. Today, everybody knows somebody . . .

A lot of kids grow up with the numbed-out emotions of survivors. Many are like their grandfathers who survived World War II and Korea, their fathers who survived Vietnam, or their mothers and grandmothers who survived sexual abuse. Survivors tend to be confused, not sure what to think, not sure how to feel, not sure whom to trust, prone to excess . . . Any of this sound familiar?

> However, those who feel this way want revenge, not apologies.—Eli

To make matters worse, most kids log too much time on the receiving end of contempt, verbal disrespect, and emotional manipulation. So a lot of kids hide the truth when they're victimized. Racked by shame and false guilt, they keep it to themselves. When a kid finally breaks the silence, it's pretty discouraging to hear an adult who treats her like dirt say, "Why didn't you come to me? I'm here for you . . ."

> Safety often becomes *something*, as opposed to a place or person. Drugs. Porn. Something.—Eli
>
> Safety is an illusion.—Brian

Most kids don't even feel safe at home. For the moment, let's rule out fathers and mothers who assault their children. Let's just think about parents who break their children's hearts. The specter of emotional abuse—some call it emotional incest— haunts young people.

> *The song was called "Los Angeles" and the words and images were so harsh and bitter that the song would reverberate in my mind for days. The images, I later found out, were personal and no one I knew shared them. The images I had were of people being driven mad by living in the city. Images of parents who were so hungry and unfulfilled that they ate their own children. Images of people, teenagers my own age, looking up from the asphalt and being blinded by the sun. These images stayed with me even after I left the city. Images so violent and malicious that they seemed to be my only point of reference for a long time afterwards. After I left.*
> —*nineteen-year-old Bret Easton Ellis*[2]

[1] U.S. Census Bureau, Vital Statistics Report, October 1998.

[2] Bret Easton Ellis, *Less Than Zero* (New York: Simon and Schuster, 1985), pp. 207-208.

Ellis was wrong about one thing. The images he described were not just personal. When I read this passage to people in their teens and twenties, they know exactly what he means.

So, if kids feel alone, afraid, unsafe, then . . .

Kids feel unsafe emotionally, intellectually, physically, relationally, spiritually. People who feel unsafe flinch every time they hear a loud noise. We can't do much about the loud noises. We'd better do something about the unsafe feelings.

Create safe environments. Start by creating an environment where your child feels safe because she *is* safe. You can't prevent random acts of violence any more than you can keep a plane from crashing into your house. It can happen anywhere. A seventeen-year-old from my middle-class neighborhood was shot dead by a retired U.S. Air Force colonel from the same neighborhood. The two pulled off the road in rush-hour traffic after someone cut someone off and they exchanged angry hand gestures; the boy got out of his car and moments later lay dead. The colonel was acquitted by a jury of his peers who believed he felt threatened by the admittedly angry but unarmed teenager pounding on his car window. Just driving away from the dispute apparently never occurred to either of them.

The response of local kids was basically, *What did you expect? It's open season on teenagers.* I feel sad about that.

I can't build a wall around my child, even in the suburbs or a small town. What I *can* do is become an advocate for kids. I can refuse to let any adult disrespect or mistreat a kid when I'm around.

I can resist the temptation to tease. Kids are easy targets for teasing. Many are physically awkward. Most are verbally impulsive. Their voices crack. They walk around wearing targets, front and back. Think back to your own childhood. Any bad experiences with teasing in your baby book? There are in mine.

When I was ten or thereabouts I was involved in a baseball accident. The people in the stands could see we were going to collide, Ronnie Poppel and me, and nobody could do a thing about it. We were so intent on catching the fly ball we neither saw nor heard anything else in the world. I suspect it looked like slow motion to the crowd, but we were both on a dead run when we collided. He flew one way and I flew the other. I was bigger but Ronnie was angular, and I came away from the transaction with a mangled upper lip. The only doctor on call that afternoon was an obstetrician, a nice man I'm sure, but no Michelangelo when it came to stitching upper lips. So I came away from that transaction with an impressive scar. Being still fifteen years away from my first convincing mustache, I wore that scar through the rest of my boyhood. It's not a huge, gross scar, just crooked and a little bumpy. Maybe it made kissing slightly more interesting. Maybe not. But an adult, whose opinion I valued more than my own, called me "Harelip" off and on for several years. I couldn't have been more humiliated. Of course, there was absolutely nothing I could do about it but feel self-conscious—and add that indignity to the list of reasons that person was not to be fully trusted. And then feel guilty for not trusting.—jb

Teasing is tough on kids. So pick on someone your own size. Better yet, don't tease. See if anybody complains.

Tell your own stories. If I know anything, I know how to make a room as safe as it can be. I'm not saying I have the heart to make every room safe, only that I know how. Ready? Here it is: In order for a room to be safe, somebody has to go first. Going first means abandoning the party line and telling my real story. It means coming clean. Making a room safe is as simple and as complicated as that.

Parents ask, "How much should I tell my child?" In my opinion, before it's over, you should tell your child everything.

> Ooh, I don't know. Everything? What if he thinks that means it's okay for him to do some of the things I wish I could take back?

Yeh. Everything. They won't think it's okay for them. They'll understand better how you got so screwed up.

> We held a "Parenting Adolescents" class at my church and one of the classes featured a panel of high school students. A parent stood up and asked if she should tell her kids she had premarital sex in college. The response was a unanimous "yes" from the students—so that kids know she's a real human being who makes mistakes and can thus relate to her, and so they could learn from *her* mistakes as well.—Alice

So, tell them everything. I am. Bit by bit, as Kate got older, I told her more and more. She knows the stories behind most of my stories.

What she doesn't know, because she doesn't need to know, is the *details* of those stories. The details are useless to her. But, as my 12-Step friends say, admitting the exact *nature* of my wrong is quite useful—to her and to me. The exact nature of my wrong is far more instructive than the details could possibly be. Kate might tell you I crossed the line here or there with too much detail and she would be right. Learning *how* to tell the truth of my story is taking some time.

Some of my stories aren't a bit sordid. It's probably worth mentioning that Kate is most comfortable with the fantasy that she was conceived by artificial insemination. She shudders to think Susan and I ever, you know, *did it*. When Kate spins that little yarn for friends and family, and we give her The Smile, she feigns a body-racking case of the willies. But she loves it. The Smile tells her more about us than details of our sex life ever could.

When trying to determine how to tell your story, consider what will be most helpful for each child—they're all different, you know. And for heaven's sake, don't vent. Venting for the sake of getting something off your chest so you'll feel better may be nearly as harmful as withholding. Tell your stories carefully and on purpose.

I would hate to assume you're actually considering telling your story just because I suggested it.

So let me suggest it again. Tell the story. It'll cost you something, sure. But not as much as you're paying now to keep it a secret.

Frederick Buechner is one of my favorite writers. No one does what he does any better than Buechner does what he does.

I have come to believe that by and large the human family all has the same secrets, which are both very telling and very important to tell. They are telling in the sense that they tell what is perhaps the central paradox of our condition—that what we hunger for perhaps more than anything else is to be known in our full humanness, and yet that is often just what we also fear more than anything else. It is important to tell at least from time to time the secret of who we truly and fully are—even if we tell it only to ourselves—because otherwise we run the risk of losing track of who we truly and fully are. . . . It is important to tell our secrets too because it makes it easier that way to see where we have been in our lives and where we are going. It also makes it easier for other people to tell us a secret or two of their own, and exchanges like that have a lot to do with what being a family is all about and what being human is all about.[3]

If you're hungry to be known in your full humanness, if you want to see where you've been in your life and where you're going, if you want to make it easier for your child to tell you a secret or two of his own, then go first.

Yeh, but what if he uses it against me?

He won't. Not if you don't use truth against him. And that, of course, is the trick. Most of us appreciate the spirit of the Golden Rule even if we can't recall where we learned it. *Do unto others as you would have them do unto you.* At its simplest, it's about fairness.

I thought it was do unto others *before* they do unto you. No wait, I remember: The Golden Rule is, he who has the gold, rules.

Go ahead, be cynical. That's the best way to raise cynical kids. With very little effort, the children of cynics can be trained to distrust the parents who raised them. So, that's something to look forward to in your old age.

I'm not suggesting foolishness. If your kid is in trouble already—if he lies, cheats, steals, covers up, and uses misdirecting accusations like: "You don't trust me!"—in that case, there's a lot of makeup work to do.

Even then, I think the Golden Rule applies. In smooth sailing or rough waters, our kids tend to treat us as they feel they've been treated.

It's possible to silence a child with verbal force so that, instead of responding in kind, he goes *inside* with it. The child's perceptions are the determining factor here. It doesn't matter how I think I'm treating my daughter. Her reactions are based on how *she* thinks I'm treating her.

This isn't theoretical for me. I'm a word guy. I know how to use words that heal. I also know how words can make razor-thin cuts in people I care about. My verbal weapon of choice has always been sarcasm. I don't rage or cuss. I cut.

When I began to understand the damage my sarcasm did to my family, I started working at

[3] Frederick Buechner, *Telling Secrets* (New York: HarperCollins, 1991), pp 2-3.

being a kinder, gentler father and husband. Here's the painful thing. For years after I stopped using sarcasm habitually, my daughter still thought of me as sarcastic, still flinched and blanched in ordinary conversation, when I was just trying to be funny . . . or ironic (Hey, the kids are supposed to love that!). I'm not sure we're done with it *yet*. I'm frustrated about that but I know beyond a shadow of doubt that we'll be done when Kate is no longer afraid. Not a day sooner.

> **Sticks and stones may break my bones, but words can break my heart.**

It's common for kids who've done the wrong thing, made bad choices, screwed up—pick your euphemism—to shut down just when they most need to open up. Unfortunately, this is also common among kids who've been hurt in ways that aren't readily apparent: victims of sexual and emotional assault. I can't explain it. I can only report seeing it over and over and over . . . especially in victims of sexual abuse. They didn't do anything wrong, but they think, feel, and believe they did. They have no reason to hide, but they do. I've also seen withdrawal in kids who lost parents or grandparents to death or divorce. They take on responsibility for things they had nothing to do with and, like Edgar Allen Poe's *Telltale Heart*, they can't stop until they've been properly punished. Unlike Poe's character, they can't turn themselves in because they didn't do anything. So, they act as judge, jury, and jailer. Their punishment isn't swift but it's sure.

I knew a high school senior who seemed to be doing everything he could to undermine his graduation into the rest of life. He blew off school, baited his father and stepmother until they exploded, and stole from his employer in a way that was sure to get him caught. When we got to the bottom of it, it had nothing to do with a fear of graduating from high school. He recalled three overpowering events in early childhood. First, his parents separated. A few months later, his grandfather died. Finally, his dog died. Surveying the wreckage of his five-year-old life, he drew an important conclusion: *When I love someone, they go away.*

Simple, clean, direct, wrong. But for the next twelve years he lived as if it were true. He distanced himself from his father, refused to get close to his stepmother, kept his friendships shallow and disposable.

Then one of those friends—closer than most—up and died on him. And that was that. The kid just spun out of control.

It took a long time to get there but, when he finally told me his terrible secret, I asked a few questions:

"When you were five, did you really have anything to do with the divorce of your parents or the death of your grandfather or your dog?"

"No."

"In the twelve years since then, have you *acted* as if those things were your fault?"

"Yes."

"Does that make sense to you now?"

"No."

"Hmmm . . . me neither. So, what do you wanna do about that?"

He wanted to change his mind. He decided to opt back into life. We brought his dad into the mix and they hashed out a lot of complicated issues. They told the story to his stepmother. He made restitution to his former employer. He squared things with the school and did the work necessary to graduate with his class.

He got his life back.

Here's the thing. If a kid can't *say* it—whatever *it* is—it doesn't go away. But it does go somewhere. It goes into aggressive behavior, or withdrawal, or eating disorders, or inappropriate risk-taking, or acting out sexually, or people-pleasing, or numbing the pain with alcohol or any of a zillion drugs of choice. No kidding. If a kid isn't communicating on a significant emotional level, it doesn't matter how calm things look on the surface. Underneath, there are riptides that will, sooner or later, drag her out to sea. If she doesn't get her feet on something solid, even the strongest swimmer will succumb eventually. It's the law. Like it or lump it.

A couple of more things.

Don't back down in a crisis. Be an advocate for your child. Don't fight his fights but, if your kid is ever victimized, be his champion. We teach children that adults are always right. We know that isn't so. But because adults are so much more powerful than kids, in a showdown the kid doesn't have a fighting chance. In the middle of a verbal hammering, who can blame a kid if he covers up and retreats to his corner? Not me.

But retreat doesn't mean defeat. He may just be cutting his losses. That's not what I want my child to do. If she's right, I want her to win. I won't hijack her conflict and make it mine. But I'll throw all my resources behind her. And if I was the one who did her wrong, I'll surrender, take my medicine like an adult, make amends, and do everything in my power to move on. I promise.

I've seen a lot of people let fear, anger, embarrassment, and self-will keep them from getting to the real story—*the story behind the story*. Sometimes it's embarrassing but relatively harmless. Once, when Kate was an infant, I couldn't get her to stop crying in a restaurant. I tried cooing and cajoling and—finally—firmness. After a few minutes, I stood up from the table, a little bent out of shape, to take her outside until she calmed down. When I released the top of the high chair, she stopped crying immediately, not because I picked her up but because the high chair stopped pinching her leg. Duh.

More recently—this year if you must know—I was pretty unsympathetic about Kate's college poverty. Don't get me wrong: She's always been thrifty beyond my wildest hopes. But in her senior year, she was struggling to stay even. All of a sudden she was broke all the time. She wasn't eating as well as I thought she should.

Me: "Have you heard the new Dave Matthews album?"

She (sighing): "Um, not yet. Couldn't afford it yet."

Well, too bad, I thought. If she has to learn not to waste money, pain is an excellent tutor.

FOR MORE ON EMOTIONAL VOCABULARY, GO TO PAGE **141**.

I don't know what I was thinking. I *wasn't* thinking, actually. She's always been a great money-manager; nothing had changed. When I finally got the story behind the story, it wasn't Kate's problem, it was mine. I've never been accused of being overly clever with a calculator. I'd underestimated Kate's legitimate senior year expenses by about 20 percent. She was broke because I didn't pay attention . . . again. I feel bad about that. I also feel bad—worse really—that I poor-mouthed her so much that Kate didn't feel free to identify my mistake and ask for help. I'd like to have do-overs on that.

I remember do-overs! When we were kids, if somebody made a mistake in marbles or jacks or hopscotch, we gave them do-overs. I could sure use some of that now.

Here's how it nets out. Find out what your kid thinks happened before you rush to judgment. I'm not saying you'll find your child was right. I'm only saying you won't know until you've heard and understood the whole story. It's that Golden Rule thing again.

Lest I lead anyone astray, here's another place where I'm certainly not recommending foolishness. I'm just saying, have the conversation; do the work.

Finally: Be a champion for kids.

Q: How do people move up in organizations these days?

A: People move up by being problem-solvers.

Be a problem-solver for your kid, but learn to do it without hijacking the kid's pain. Or his process. This is serious. A highly involved, empathetic parent will take the wind right out of a kid's sail if she steals his problem. This is the balance between Champion and Benevolent Dictator.

Benevolent Dictators are still Dictators.

The Dictator takes his child's pain too personally and wades in to fix things. "They can't do that to us!" Well, they didn't do it to *us*; they did it to *him*. And if the Dictator jumps in to rescue by throwing his weight around, he's about to do it to him again. Nobody wants that.

The Champion, on the other hand, enters the fray *with* her child: training, empowering, supporting. Being your child's Champion prepares her to stand up for herself when you're not around—which is only a matter of time. So learn to see immediate problems as elements of a bigger challenge: How do I prepare this person for life in the real world? What does she need to know about

FOR MORE ON DO-OVERS, GO TO PAGE **172**.

herself? About perceptions? About communication? About negotiation? About decision-making? About solving her own problems? One day soon, she needs to know all those things or people will take advantage of her. If I don't help her learn them, who will?

🧍 What's the most significant thing you read or thought about in this chapter?

🧍 Why do you think that's so significant?

🧍 What do you think you might want to do about that?

🧍 Don't take my word for it. What did you read here that's worth checking with a kid?

FOR MORE ON SELF ASSESSMENT, GO TO PAGE **139**; FOR PERCEPTIONS GO TO PAGE **123**; NEGOTIATION, PAGE **121**; DECISION-MAKING, PAGE **56**.

Angry and Getting Used to It

3.4

Anger is the

cheapest drug

I know.

—Brian

> I cannot control the way the world is run, the way others treat me, the hand I have been dealt, but I can damn well control the way I treat others (especially those who least expect it). —Kate

> My mom was an unhealthy model for me in terms of dealing with anger. I was constantly walking on eggshells, in fear of her irrational outbursts. I consequently have a hard time expressing my own anger because I know how my mom's anger made me feel (like crap, like I couldn't do anything right), because I'm afraid it'll jeopardize my relationships, and because I'm afraid of being irrational. —Alice

> Anger is the cheapest drug I know. —Brian

Our kids are doing a generational slow burn.

> Don't tell me you haven't noticed. Their anger comes out as contempt, outbursts of rage, mean-spirited humor, stealing, vandalism, and every once in a while, shocking acts of violence.

Urban dwellers are uncomfortably familiar with these things. I know a young man whose little brother was the fifty-eighth child killed in Chicago the year the paper kept a running total. He lived and died in the Henry Horner Projects—the place described in the book and film *There Are No Children Here.* He was shot in the back, reportedly a case of mistaken identity in a drug dispute.

Across town, Lane High School is a magnet for four thousand of Chicago's brightest students.

Kids declare a major when they test into Lane. It's a tough, exciting academic environment. Things are exciting outside too. Lane started after-school programs so students would trickle out of the building instead of exiting all at once. The programs are innovative and enriching but that's not why they started. They started because of drive-by shootings targeting who-knows-who and endangering the lives of hundreds of middle-adolescents.

The circumstances at Lane—positive and negative—never make the news outside Chicago. What made news as the 21st century turned were suburban and small town conspiracies and shootings that spread like buckshot across the nation. It was described as a wave of student-on-student violence. I'm afraid it was big news because the killers and most of their victims were Anglo children from middle-class homes who acted without reference to drugs or rock and roll (although a shooting in Pearl, Mississippi, was accompanied by whispered reports of Satanism, and sex was involved in the Texas murder of a suburban high school girl by two kids on their way to U.S. military academies).

> If you ask me, these are the acts of angry people. It's more complicated than that, but anger is a prime motivator for millions of young Americans. Fraternity hazing is an anger binge. *They did it to me when I was initiated and now somebody's going to pay. Not the ones who did it to me, maybe, but somebody.*

I think anger is the drive behind a lot of the violence in organized sports. There was an angry ritual at my high school thirty years ago. On the last day of football practice, for as long as anyone could remember, after the coaches left the field, all the seniors lined up between the goal posts and made the younger boys pass through them. It was the seniors' last chance to express their appreciation for their teammates. As a sophomore I watched older boys beat the hell out of younger boys. I recall Charlie Pope on top of me, pounding on my face mask before letting me up. As a junior I got off pretty easy because I was a starter. We'd had a frustrating season but, apparently, nobody was too frustrated with me.

Thirteen months later, Ted Strauss and I were co-captains of the team. It was the last day of practice, but this year our final game would be for the state championship. The State Championship! In twenty-four hours we would be in the locker room used by the Florida State Seminoles, preparing to go out in front of a capacity crowd, to win or lose the state title.

Before our last practice the seniors had a brief discussion about the value of tradition versus teamwork. As the tide turned toward teamwork, a couple of guys expressed frustration that they wouldn't have the chance to do to someone else what was done to them as underclassmen. Ultimately, though, no one wanted that particularly twisted revenge more than he wanted a state championship. So we didn't do it. When practiced ended, the coaches left the field as they did every year. We called the team into a huge huddle and churned the worn-out sod with our cleats, and hollered and cheered and mainlined adrenaline like the junkies we were. The scrum ended with a mighty shout and we all ran through the goalposts together.

As far as I know, the tradition died that day. The next day, we won the state title.

I'm not saying organized sports are inherently flawed, I'm saying *people* are—or at least I am. The anger many of us felt in those days didn't just go away because we chose to not beat up our younger teammates. It went somewhere else. I'm glad we didn't generate more anger for those younger guys by victimizing them. But that is what we do on a regular basis in this culture. We do the things that were done to us, the things that made us angry and crazy, and our victims do those things too and it just about never ends until somebody asks, "Is this gonna help us win the state championship? Cuz if it isn't, I don't think we should do it."

I think sexual violence springs from anger. A lot of us come to see sex as intimate power because we've been overpowered sexually. I've had the solemn duty of helping quite a few people begin dealing with sexual assault. It's disconcerting how many of them—the *victims* —learned to use sex as a weapon. There's something about us . . .

There's something that moves us to do to others, not as we would have them do to us, but as someone before them *did* to us. The barely conscious knee-jerk reaction is not: "That sucked, I would never put anybody through that." The knee-jerk is, "That sucked, I want somebody else to suffer like I suffer" or "That sucked, maybe I'll feel stronger if I'm on the delivering end of the pain instead of the receiving end." I don't get it. I've seen it over and over. I've even done it. But I don't get it.

In the end, I think anger springs from fear more than anything. Remember the formula from Psychology 101? Fear = Fight or Flight.

Fear is a frequent visitor. — Brian

People in danger seem about as likely to lash out as to withdraw. And the lashing (or the withdrawal for that matter) may be about something with no obvious connection to the fear hidden beneath it. That's why kids can do angry, violent things and, when asked why they acted like that, say with real conviction, "I don't know."

When grownups get caught, I think our version of "I don't know" comes out something like "I wasn't thinking." Adults have a hard time saying, "I don't know." What's even harder to admit is, down deep, we *did* know what we were doing but we were powerless to stop ourselves.

I'm not recommending a game of amateur psychology to figure out why your family members are mad. Do that and you'll find out exactly why they're angry, at least at that moment. But I'm quite interested in Stephen Covey's notion of seeking first to understand:

If I were to summarize in one sentence the single most important principle I have learned in the field of interpersonal relations, it would be this: Seek first to understand, then to be understood.[1]

[1] Stephen R. Covey, *The Seven Habits of Highly Effective People* (New York: Simon and Schuster, 1989), p. 237.

If what's behind all this anger were obvious, it would be easy. It's not. So I have to work to understand what's beneath my child's anger (and mine).

A couple of years ago, I had a nasty case of hives—red, angry welts covered my torso, backside, and thighs. Not too good for my sex life. For six months, various and sundry medics treated the hives with various and sundry medications, all to no effect if you don't count acute cotton-mouth and chronic drug-induced depression. Finally, someone treated the systemic problem underneath the hives and they just went away. Red, angry welts are obvious and, therefore, attention-grabbing. But I want to deal with what's really wrong. Anger is a symptom; fear is a systemic problem.

I wish I'd understood this better when Kate was young.

So, if our kids are angry and getting used to it, then . . .

Create safe places. Our kids are plenty angry because they're plenty scared. We have to take the idea of safety a step further by creating sanctuaries where kids are safe from judgment, danger, and inhumanity.

Kate may remember this differently, but I don't recall ever arguing at our family table. We played with food, made jokes, told stories, and recounted the adventures and misadventures of the day. We didn't do much problem-solving or decision-making and we didn't fight. The table was (and is) a safe place to just *be*.

FOR MORE ON SELF-ASSESSMENT, GO TO PAGE **139**.

> If you want to delight your children and scandalize your mother, after you finish eating some night, casually peel an orange and squeeze the colorful side of the peel about two inches from a candle flame. In my opinion, this tiny fireworks display makes oranges nearly twice as useful as before.

Just *being* is good for digestion. There's plenty of time and there are many good locations to unearth and solve problems. Why not create sanctuaries for being? A bedroom, the kitchen table, the family automobile. Suit yourself. Just designate a place where everyone checks their guns at the door.

Become a safe person. Anger, judging, grudge-holding, coldness. These are attributes of unsafe people.

> Most of us teach our children not to take unnecessary risks. What a pity when a child looks in the eyes of his parent and thinks, *I'd better not go there alone.*

Which leads to the unpleasant admission that I'm dealing (slowly) with anger of my own. Which is also to admit I'm afraid and I withdraw and withhold myself from my family and I lash out with sarcasm. Which is to admit I'm still not a safe person.

I'm not saying I withdraw and withhold and lash out every day—not anymore. But I've done all these habitually and, along the way, learned that just because I didn't raise my voice doesn't mean my daughter didn't feel yelled at. Do you know what I'm saying here? I'm saying my angry daughter was raised by an angry man who is very (very) slowly learning the value of a fair fight, an honest admission of fear, an open confession of failure, a genuine apology.

Becoming a safe person for my family is a long process in my life. I think they'll tell you I've come a long way. I think they'll agree I have a long way to go.

Don't frustrate kids needlessly. Did I mention I'm a sucker for the Bible? It started way back when and I love the Book. But, well, here are a few words I could do without:

> Fathers, don't exasperate your children by coming down hard on them. Take them by the hand and lead them in the way of the Master. . . . Parents, don't come down too hard on your children or you'll crush their spirits.[2]

Aarrgh! I can't tell you how often I've come down hard on my daughter and how seldom I've taken her by the hand and led her in the way of the Master. I think I've erred most often by failing to get enough information, judging by appearances, jumping to conclusions—stupid stuff like that. I've also made mountain ranges out of molehills, ridiculous overreactions that said way more about me than her.

[2] *The Message* New Testament (Colorado Springs: NavPress, 1994), pp. 409 and 426.

FOR MORE ON SAFETY, GO TO PAGE **108**.

Thank God her spirit isn't crushed. But I'm afraid her spirit is broken toward me to some degree. She's an adult now and the more I treat her like an adult, the more chances I have to heal the damage I inflicted by coming down too hard.

Of course, this is not to say I shouldn't have *come down* at all.

> Here it comes. Is this gonna be one of those word plays you're so fond of? Everybody pay attention, he's gonna make an obscure reference . . .

Coming down is a way of talking about *condescending*, an interesting term that sounds negative on the face of it. But it ain't necessarily so. Let me put the best spin on it. Making a point about what he called the *divine condescension,* C. S. Lewis wrote about how some humans descend into sympathy with animals and how "adult minds (but only the best of them) can descend into sympathy with children."[3] I like that because I think there's a kind of coming down—not *on* kids but *to* them and *with* them—that's not negative at all. It is, as Lewis has it, *sympathy:* feeling what the other person feels.

So what do your kids feel? I don't know, ask them. Whether things are going well or badly, engage your children in a bit of emotional recall by asking them to describe their feelings:

Adult: What happened to your knee?
Child: I tripped.
Adult: Ouch! That must've hurt!
Child: Not too bad. I'm okay.

Adult: Was anybody watching? (Because the adult knows the child believes people are always watching.)
Child: Yeh. I felt like an idiot.
Adult (resisting the urge to say, "Don't say that! You're not an idiot!"): Like how did you feel like an idiot?
Child: I just feel like a dork, always tripping and stuff.
Adult: I hate it when that happens. Did people laugh at you?
Child: Of course. When Martina dropped her books, everybody cracked up. I felt so sorry for her.
Adult (careful to identify with the feelings but not to hijack the moment): I closed my coat in the car door one time. My mom started driving off and I was screaming and pounding on the window.
Child: What did you do?
Adult: I was so embarrassed. She stopped right away and got out all scared and everything.
Child: No way!
Adult: Yeh. We picked up my books and she just kept apologizing. It really scared her.
Child: Did anybody see?
Adult: I don't know. I thought everybody saw. Later, one of my friends said, "You're so lucky. My mom would've yelled at me if that happened."
Child: Why? It was an accident!
Adult: Yep, it was . . . like you tripping this morning.
Child: Only funnier!

[3] C. S. Lewis, *Miracles* (New York: Macmillan, 1947), p. 111.

FOR MORE ON HELPING KIDS EXPRESS THEIR FEELINGS, GO TO PAGE 139.

> Okay, you made that up! Nothing ever happens that smoothly.

Okay, so I made that up. But it's exactly the kind of process I've seen my wife go through with our daughter. I've even pulled it off a few times myself. It's a process of acknowledging feelings instead of discounting them. It's about identifying with the feelings and putting them in a larger context without diminishing the immediate circumstances. And it's possible only if the adult remembers what embarrassment felt like when she was young.

On our best days we know what our children feel because we felt it ourselves in a life that may seem long ago and far away but which, nonetheless, connects us to each other. I admit I haven't done too many things on purpose in my life, but I did this: When I decided to work with kids, I decided never to forget what it felt like to *be* a kid. That requires periodic trips down memory lane, sometimes through neighborhoods I'd rather not visit. But I swear it's made me a better youth worker, a better father, a better human. If nothing else (and there's a lot else) these trips remind me how frustrating it already is to be a child—especially an adolescent. So, if I could help it, why would I make it harder on a kid?

Stop playing zero sum games. The term *zero sum game* describes an exchange where one person must lose in order for another to win. The term comes from Game Theory, the interdisciplinary field that tries to explain and predict people's behavior in negotiations and conflicts.[4] In a zero sum game there's never enough for everyone.

> Poker is a zero sum game, Monopoly isn't. In poker, one person takes the whole pot and everybody else makes excuses. In Monopoly, there are degrees of winning and losing. This is why my wife won't let me play poker with the children.

There are four possible outcomes in human transactions:

Win/Win. We come out even. If I sell you a good car at a fair price, we end up with win/win.

Win/Lose. I win and you lose. If I bet you twenty bucks the Jets will beat the Saints and I happen to know the Jets already beat the Saints in an earlier time zone, we end up with win/lose.

Lose/Win. I lose and you win. If I give you money to buy lunch and you spend it all on your lunch and tell me there wasn't enough for both of us, we end up with lose/win.

Lose/Lose. We both lose. If we can't agree to split the cookie and end up crumbling it all over the floor, we end up with lose/lose.

On paper, you'd think everybody would work for win/win. I mean, what's not to like about that? But life isn't lived on paper.

Most of us seem able to live with win/lose for extended periods. Not that we necessarily want others to lose, but that's not our problem, is it? We're busy people—busy earning a living, making a home, looking after the needs of others. It takes effort to share the win and we're already spread pretty thin.

[4] The classic game theory text is *The Compleat Strategyst* by J.D. Williams, (New York: Dover Publications, 1954).

If I learned anything at my momma's knee, it was watch out for yourself cuz nobody else will. It's part of the culture. Looking out for number one is job number one.

The trouble is, my win/lose is a lose/win for the person on the other side. And lose/win feels terrible. One way to get more or less permanently upside down in a relationship is to let it take on the unpleasant flavor of lose/win for the other person. Nobody is content with a lose/win relationship. Why should they be? Put anyone — parent or kid — in that position and, sooner or later, one way or another, they'll get it back.

Foot-dragging is a favorite ploy for kids who believe they're stuck in a lose/win relationship.

> **Adult:** Listen mister. I want this kitchen spotless by the time I get back. I want every cup and plate washed and put away. You read me?
> *Silence.*
> **Adult:** I said, *Do you read me?*
> **Child:** I read you! Cups and plates put away. Fine!
> *Time passes. The adult returns and surveys the kitchen.*
> **Adult:** Excuse me, but I thought I told you to clean the kitchen. Why isn't the counter clean?
> **Child:** Excuse me but you didn't say *counter.*

That kind of passive-aggressive behavior is maddening to the adult and not that much fun for the kid. It's more emotional than rational. It's an attempt to pull even in the game. Of course, I've seen it work the other way as well. I've seen harried, under-appreciated adults—teachers, retail managers, parents—glaze over with an attitude that seems to say, "I may not be able to win but that doesn't mean I can't make you lose."

Now, take Game Theory home with you and you've got a significant diagnostic tool.

I've mediated a lot of family conflicts and quite a few friend-to-friend disagreements. Everybody's mad and hurt and afraid. They've concluded they can't solve their problems without help and they hope I'm it. I agree to meet with them separately and, as each one tells the whole story from his or her point of view, it usually becomes obvious they're saying things to me they haven't said to each other. Things look bad. But how bad?

I outline the four game outcomes and ask, "Can I assume lose/win is not okay with you?" It turns out I can always assume that.

> **Me:** How about win/lose? Can you live with win/lose?
> **Kid:** No, win/lose doesn't work either. My mom doesn't have to suffer, *I* just don't wanna hafta lose in order for her to win.

In this case I know we're not far from reconciliation. I ask the kid to outline what he thinks would create a win/win outcome. Then I repeat the process with his mom and, assuming things look more or less the same from her point of view, get them face to face to say to each other what they said to me. It's time-consuming but not that complicated.

But sometimes, when I ask if win/lose is okay, one or the other says, "Absolutely. Win/lose is perfect for me. Way better than win/win. How do I get there?"

This is a different problem.

Me: Are you saying win/win doesn't work for you? Are you saying your mom has to lose in order for you to win?

Kid: If you heard me say I can't win unless my mom loses, you heard me right.

Me: So, are you saying you're so mad you'd rather have a lose/lose than a win/win because if she doesn't lose you can't win?

Kid: Read my lips. This is what I'm saying: If I have to lose to be sure she loses, I'll live with that. The important thing is for her to lose.

Me: Oh.

That's a pretty serious amount of anger.

My next task is finding out what created that much anger. I know it's gonna be awhile before I get the parties face to face. But that's not to say it can't be worked out. The lose/lose gambit has been the wake-up call for quite a few parents. They knew there were significant problems, sure, but they had no idea how far apart they were. Once they understand how high the stakes have risen, parents usually sober up and come to the table for real.

At the end of the day, disagreements are seldom about someone being all wrong and someone else being all right. Disagreements most often spring from different perceptions—different ways of seeing the same thing. I arranged to meet Susan in the lobby of a hotel last weekend, not realizing there were two lobbies, one on each side of the street. I'm less than thrilled with the designers of the hotel, but that doesn't mean Susan was in the wrong lobby. It was the first lobby she came to; why would she look for another? What kind of lame-brained hotel has multiple lobbies? Come to think of it, how many more lobbies could there be that we didn't find?

That's the thing about perceptions. Two people can share the same experience and come out with vastly different perceptions.

Two people emerge from a theater.
She: Wow.
He: You can say that again.
She: I'm stunned.
He: Me too. In fact, I'm outraged.
She: Wait a minute. Outraged?
He: Yeh. I can't believe we wasted three hours watching people get naked and drown.
She: That's so not the point of that. I, I, did we see the same film?
He: I thought so. Hey, do you have hay fever or something? I thought I heard you sniffling in there and now your eyes are all red.
She: I think you'd better take me home.
He: What! What'd I say?

So maybe that's a little obvious. But any time two or more people get together you can bet there are real differences in perception. Sometimes those differences turn into conflicts. Thoughtful listening can turn most conflicts over perceptions to win/win.

Example: Susan is a nester, I'm a wanderer. Don't get me wrong, once the nest is secure, Susan can out-wander me. It's just that, if I've got a motel reservation and it's guaranteed for late arrival, I don't care when I get there. Susan likes to visualize where she'll be sleeping. She likes to get settled in just a bit and then go out. She doesn't insist, it's just her preference. You know what? It just doesn't matter to me. I have no real preference about that most of the time. So why wouldn't I put myself in Susan's place and go check in at the motel before I start wandering? No reason at all.

Example: Kate is a slow starter. She finishes big at night; anybody can tell you that. But she likes to ease into the morning. Not a lot of conversation; not a lot of food; not a lot of eye contact. I, on the other hand, tend to shift into high gear right off the line. The minute I get up—well, the minute I come out of the bathroom—I'm about as good as I'll be all day. You want early morning conversation? I'm your man. Bagels and Diet Coke? Let me get my keys. What? You want to spend some time alone? Oh . . . okay. Whatever . . . The thing is, I'm the kind of extrovert who can enjoy those activities with a total stranger. That being the case, do I really need to engage Kate in her least relationally productive hours? Of course not.

When it comes down to it, what actually *happened* is seldom in question. What's usually at stake is what we think it means and what we think we'll do about it. That's a judgment call every time. Why would I insist you see things my way and my way only? Who died and made me king?

> I like that Ray Bradbury quote about perceptions. How'd that go again? "And isn't that what life is all about, the ability to go around back and come up inside other people's heads to look out at the damned fool miracle and say: oh so that's how you see it!? Well, now, I must remember that."

When we treat children in our lives with that kind of respect, they have less to be afraid of. If our kids have less to fear, they have less to be angry about. I think you can take it from there.

- What's the most significant thing you read or thought about in this chapter?

- Why do you think that's so significant?

- What do you think you might want to do about that?

- Don't take my word for it. What did you read here that's worth checking with a kid?

Without Feathers

3.5

We're always hearing about the decline of society, the death of the ozone, the extinction of species, death of the oceans. What is there to hope for?

—Kate

We're always hearing about the decline of society, the death of the ozone, the extinction of species, death of the oceans. What is there to hope for?—Kate

Emily Dickinson wrote, "Hope is the thing with feathers . . ."[1] Woody Allen called one of his books *Without Feathers*. For a lot of modern kids, "without feathers" about sums it up. They don't expect things to get much better for them and they'll be surprised if things don't get considerably worse.

Strangelove Reproduction: Having children to make up for the fact that one no longer believes in the future.
—**Douglas Coupland** [2]

Part of it, I think, is they've seen so many of us—their parents—grow old and die years before we stop breathing.

We regale them with stories about how things were different when we were young. We burned with purpose and passion; we *did* something when we were young. We did something about civil rights and the war—*The War*. Our muddy, bloody skirmishes in the Mekong Delta or the Gulf of Tonkin or Kent State or Chicago. And for the most part they listen politely, or at least they don't say much. But they wonder what happened to the fire.

[1] Woody Allen, *Without Feathers* (New York: Warner Books, 1976), copyright page.
[2] Douglas Coupland, *Generation X* (New York: St. Martin's Press, 1991), p. 135.

How could we be so vital and alive back then and so dull and workaday now? How could we

trade passion for a European car? Sure, we elected a president who's our age and just like us. So what? What have we done lately, *personally*, to make the world better?

Try getting a straight answer to *that*.

Adults no longer behave like adults. We have no role models; they're talking about sex and therapy and substance abuse, just like us.
—*Melissa Hughes, 22, in* **Rolling Stone,**
May 28, 1998, page 96

My father always tells me, "No matter what you see wrong in this country, you're still lucky." In part, that's true. I've never had to starve a day in my life. But because I start from that level, I expect more.
—*Tony Dinh, 23, in* **Rolling Stone,**
May 28, 1998, page 151

Our children have no feathers because they're growing up in a dangerous world that has less to do with nuclear weapons than handguns; less to do with the cold war than the war on drugs; less to do with finding a way to make a living than with making a life *worth* living.

I want a life that is a little bit less ordinary. I know what I don't want. I don't want a job in a bank, living in the suburbs, driving a minivan.
—*Jessica Ridenour, 22, in* **Rolling Stone,**
May 28, 1998, page 93

Like us just a few years ago, our children are looking for alternatives. A new communalism is growing. It's much more practical than Utopian. I think it's the extension of patterns they learned in adolescence when, in the absence of an adult to lend a hand, they raised each other as best they could. The food court was the kitchen table where they broke bread and listened to each other's stories. The city parks were the front stoops where they joked and watched the world go by. They met behind strip malls and on street corners, counseled each other on telephones, and called for help on pagers. They learned to administer drugs for the relief of all manner of pain, and more than a few found they could make a better living as drugstore cowboys than they could ever hope to make at a McJob.

Now, growing older, they continue those patterns in extended families-of-choice, still looking after each other as best they know how, still loyal as ever through the comings and goings of their strange modern life.

As best they know how.

A young woman at one of the first Lallapalooza concerts remarked, "We're just like the hippies, except the hippies had hope."

That's the world where our children live.

So, if our kids are without feathers, then . . .

Many of the things we're talking about leave young men and women feeling aimless, directionless, hopeless. It doesn't have to be like this. We can do a number of very practical things to build hope.

Encourage perceptions of personal effectiveness. When we believe our children can act to benefit themselves and others, we tend to *treat* them as if they might be effective. In response, children become effective. When adults treat children as if they were *incapable* of acting to benefit themselves and others, children tend to remain ineffective. You do the math.

The connection is direct. When I'm effective—when what I do makes a difference—I feel hopeful.

Start creating hope right where you are by teaching the children under your care that they can do more than just about anybody gives them credit for.

Children come to understand, believe, and act on these lessons through the cunning teaching method called *praxis. Praxis* is a Greek word that means *practice* as distinguished from *theory.* "You're a big boy, you should be able to make your own bed" never trained anybody to make his bed, though it contributes nicely to the collection of shame every big boy keeps under his bed.

These are words that teach boys to make beds:

"Hey buddy, I need your help in here. Please take that side of the sheet and tuck it in right over there like I'm doing here . . . Good. Thank you. Now take the other end up to the top of the bed like I'm doing on my side. Oops! Looks like we need to tuck it in a little more at the bottom. Great. Thank you. Okay, let's do the blanket now—same as we did the sheet. Good job! Hey, have you done this before? Come over here and let me give you a hug!"

FOR MORE ON *PRAXIS* UNDER THE IDEA OF ORTHOPRAXY, GO TO PAGE **66.**

A few days of that kind of interaction and you can ask your big boy to cover for you for a day, then two, then permanently. Notice the language: it's *good job*, not *good boy*. If, God forbid, your good boy should break his arms and not be able to make a bed, he can still be a good boy and he can still do a good job at something else.

> The same training works for sweeping, straightening, dishwashing (you may wanna put away the good china for a while), dusting, laundry (you might consider retaining responsibility for delicate fabrics in the beginning), bathroom cleaning, lawn mowing, and automobile maintenance. I wouldn't offer a lug wrench or dipstick rag to a four-year-old. I wouldn't withhold them from a ten-year-old.

You can start the training process at any time. Adjust the language to fit your personal style and the age of your partner. Here are the stages in the transfer of responsibility. They're as old as the hills; I have no idea where I learned them:

1. I do it. "Dum-de-dum-dum."
2. He watches me do it. "Hey, bud, come talk to me while I make the bed."
3. We do it together. "Hey, buddy, I need your help in here."
4. I watch him do it. "Thanks so much for making the bed today. You did a good job and that really helped me. We'll do it together tomorrow, okay?"
5. He does it. "You've gotten so good at making your bed that I'd like for that to be one of the ways you contribute to the family. That frees me up to do other things so we can all finish sooner and move on into our day. Thanks for helping the family run smoothly."

I'm not saying your big boy will get it right immediately. That's why you do it together until you know he knows.

> This is also not to say your big boy will cheerfully make his bed when he's a bigger boy. But it won't be because he doesn't know how.

The more training and responsibility you give your child in appropriate tasks, the more effective he'll feel because he actually *is* effective in those things. And you'll be the hero in his life because so much of the world doesn't believe he's capable of wiping his own nose.

> But you know he's capable because he watched you do it, then you did it together, then you watched him do it, and now he does it himself and disposes of his own tissue when he's done.

Discourage a belief in *magic*. Don't get me wrong, I enjoy a good magic show as much as the next fella. Not to mention the magic that happens when people generate good ideas, when a rock-and-roll band is really *on*, or when a dining experience couldn't be more perfect. I love magic! But I don't believe in it.

All the magic I know about is carefully designed and orchestrated to appear effortless. It really *is* an illusion. I'm not sure anything is truly effortless. Sometimes the effort is someone else's and I benefit through no work of my own. That should be called a blessing.

If you think you can, you might. If you think you can't, you won't. It's that simple. The tie-breaker is determined by trying. A lot of kids—and plenty of adults for that matter—don't try because they're already convinced they can't.

> I couldn't get promoted in this company if I was Jesus himself. Doesn't matter how much I know or how hard I work. Bottom line? The boss doesn't like me.

From a kid, it comes out in statements like *It's boring* or *The teacher doesn't like me* or *It's too hard*. If she thinks she can't, she won't. But if she thinks she can . . . Wow! The world is her oyster.

I'm not talking about feelings of *omnipotence*. I'm talking about your daughter's conviction that life can be *magical* without being *magic*. I'm talking about her belief that she can face most of life's ordinary challenges and have a pretty good shot at success. It's her belief that she can make a difference in the outcome of her own plans and efforts. These beliefs come from learning, trying, failing, trying again, and succeeding. Children who have these experiences learn to develop plans about opportunities and problems they haven't faced yet. They learn to generalize from past experiences and apply the insights they gained to what's ahead. They come to believe in the principle of cause and effect and they're not shocked when their actions produce results.

> There's a term in developmental psychology, *scaffolding*, which I think relates to this. It's when a parent helps a child with something, not by doing it themselves, and they don't just let the kids figure it out themselves. They guide and structure the experience to match the ability of the child, but leave just enough challenge so the child grows and feels as though he/she accomplishes something.—Alice

Adults contribute to this process when we train children to confront progressively more sophisticated challenges. We deepen the experience when instead of explaining what the child should be learning, we engage her in dialog to draw out what she *is* learning. Every time we contribute this kind of training to a child, what we really contribute is hope.

One of Susan's clever kindergarten students declined to help with cleanup, explaining, "I can't, Miss Susan. My hands is too small."

Of course, he was just trying to get out of work. Miss Susan assured him his hands were not too small and helped him get a grip. But many kids of all ages truly believe their hands are too small, so they're afraid to try. Someone has to guide them, train them, encourage them until they're convinced they can tackle it, whatever *it* is. When that happens, challenges and opportunities start merging for them. They may not succeed every time, but they won't fail for lack of trying.

Once kids get a grip on that, they're propelled by the thing with feathers.

FOR MORE ON MAGIC, SEE THE BOY WHO BELIEVED IN MAGIC, BY JIM HANCOCK (BERKELEY: BLUE SKY BOOKS, 1999).

What's the most significant thing you read or thought about in this chapter?

Why do you think that's so significant?

What do you think you might want to do about that?

Don't take my word for it. What did you read here that's worth checking with a kid?

Numbed Out

3.6

Our kids are

hurting, so maybe

we should *give*

them drugs.

Did you ever notice how a little snack—or a shopping trip, maybe—can take the edge off a bad afternoon? Or maybe you've found that driving fast can be a mind-altering activity, or vegging in front of the television, or nail-biting, or a couple of glasses of wine, or half an hour on the phone—whatever gets you through the night. Maybe you haven't. Maybe that's just me.

~~~

If our children have learned anything from us, it's that pain is bad. They've been miseducated into a conspiracy of addictive relationships and habits.

You know the rules: *Don't talk, don't trust, don't feel.* Is it any wonder so many grow up silent, lonely, and emotionally dead?

They'd be hard-pressed to put it into words, but a lot of kids feel responsible for the mess they're in and ashamed they can't solve their problems with the ease they believe they see in adults. But asking for help breaks the *don't trust, don't talk* rules. So kids plug away, hiding out and hoping against hope they'll get things together before they fall apart. There aren't many cries for help these days. It's more subtle than that. They just do whatever it takes to feel no pain.

For a good many years we've been fighting a war on drugs in this country. At least that's what we call it. It's a war on drugs in the same sense that the US presence in Vietnam was a war—which is to say a lot of people are suffering and dying and nobody's winning.

Somebody's going to assassinate me for this but I have good reasons for saying it, so here goes:

I think the war on drugs is a bad idea. Our kids are hurting, so maybe we should give them drugs.

Or we should help them deal with their pain.

I don't much care what you call it; addictions, life-controlling problems, compulsions, bad habits, and besetting sins are all the same to me. Feel free to split clinical, theological, and recovery hairs all you want. Meanwhile, here's a kitchen-table definition of addiction (for lack of a better term): Addiction is the habitual misuse of substances, behaviors, or relationships in the hope of feeling normal.

> Is doing too much of *anything* healthy? A big word for me is *balance.*—Eli
>
> Kids always say, "Oh, that could never happen to me" but it does and I strongly hope I'll have enough willpower to not be addicted to anything.—Ben
>
> Addictions? Got 'em.—Brian

Note the words *habitual*, *misuse*, *substances*, *behaviors*, *relationships*, and *normal*.

Addicted kids act out (or act in) *habitually*. A habit is something we do the same way every time or something we do without thinking. There's nothing *occasional* or *social* about addiction. Anne Lamott writes ironically of throwing back fifteen to twenty *social drinks* in an evening and the non-habit-forming marijuana she smoked every day for *twenty years*. Life-controlling problems are characterized by *patterns* of misuse.

Addicted kids are *misusers* of substances, behaviors, or relationships that may not be

inherently evil. There's nothing wrong with food. There's something very wrong with the way I misused food for two decades, the way I'm still tempted to misuse food.

Addicted kids misuse *substances, behaviors* **or** *relationships*. Addictive *substances*, from alcohol to Zoloft, are relatively easy to target and they're not inherently bad. Okay, maybe crack cocaine is inherently bad. I'm not aware of any constructive use for the compound and maybe there are others like it. But, by and large, the substances we misuse are benign if we don't misuse them. (I'm not making the guns-don't-kill-people-people-kill-people argument. Nobody ever accidentally held a lighter to a rock of cocaine in a glass pipe and just happened to inhale the fumes.) Guns and crack are designed with an end in mind.

> **Guns don't kill people. People kill people. Especially people with guns.**

Addictive *behaviors* are less easy to pin down. Our culture rewards *positive* compulsions. Working like crazy is a way to get ahead. The work fiend is never out of control and is always rewarded. Until the crash. Mary Bell, founder of Center for Recovering Families in Houston, says, these days, achievement is the alcohol of the corporate executive.

"People brag to me that they're working eighty hours a week, giving their lives to the company store. It's heartbreaking. Those people are prime candidates for self-destruction. The reason is simple. Our bodies will produce the pain we need to get our drugs."[1]

The boy who studies obsessively to gain approval may be in as much jeopardy as the one who smokes marijuana to take the edge off his failure. I led a group in which those two boys sat next to each other, both admitting they were out of control. The substance abuser is now recovering, building a life he can live with. I'm not so sure about the high-achiever. The props he gets from approval are very potent, especially compared to the cost of being ordinary.

Ditto beauty. The boys and girls who obsess about diet, exercise, or beauty don't get thrown in jail, but that doesn't mean their development isn't arrested.

Addictive *relationships* may be the hardest to track. Where's the line between love and co-addiction with a boy and his alcoholic girlfriend? Hard to say. Where's the line between popularity and compulsive love-seeking in a person who moves from relationship to relationship without a break? Again, a tough call.

One of the things we've failed to see in our war on drugs is that behaviors and relationships can be misused in similar patterns with results nearly identical to substance abuse. Any anorexic can tell you that.

Addicted kids do what they do to feel *normal.* We talk about getting high as if that were the point for addicts. It isn't. Getting high is a pre-addicted state. Addicted kids do their stuff so they can get through the day.

Remember the line from that Alcoholics Anonymous guy, Clancy? He said he drank the first time because the older guys asked him to join them. Then, for the next thirty-five years,

[1] quoted in *Fast Company*, October 1998, p. 118.

he drank "to feel like other men looked."

That's the bait. Like Clancy, I'm inclined to abuse money and food and adrenaline and sex and the truth because I want to *feel* like other people *look*.

In his book *Understanding the Times and Knowing What to Do,* Jimmy Lee draws a picture of what he calls "The Trap" (because people are often snared before they know what's happening).[2] It looks something like this:

Step 1: Experimenting with *It*. I discover a substance, behavior, or relational pattern that makes me feel good. Food always makes me feel better (at least for a while); driving fast always makes me feel excited (at least for a while); drinking always gets me high. I do *It*, whatever *It* is for me, to get to high from normal or low.

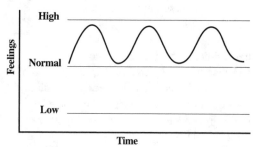

Step 2: Doing *It* socially. *It* becomes part of my social life. I may even set up personal rules for when I think *It* is appropriate: Weekends only; meal times only; never alone.

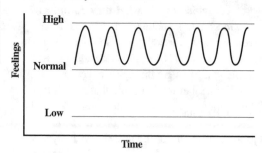

Step 3: Daily preoccupation with *It*. I'm possessed by a growing fixation and think about *It* all the time. I begin to violate my own sense of right and wrong in order to take care of *It*. Over time, the highs are not as high and the lows get much lower. *It* fails to give me the same relief *It* used to. I blow off other important things for the sake of *It*. Even if I don't do *It*, I think about *It*.

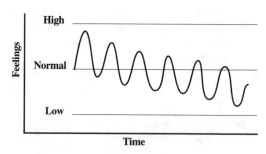

Step 4: Doing *It* to feel normal. My life is characterized by growing inflexibility. I may not make it to class or home for dinner but I will definitely find time for *It*. I do *It* just to feel normal. I take loss of dignity, broken relationships, and spiritual numbness in stride. *It* isn't a bit of fun anymore, but I need *It* to get through the day.

All this because I wanted to feel like other people look.

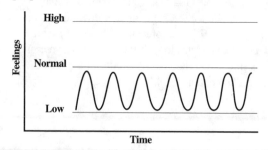

[2] Jimmy Ray Lee, *Understanding the Times and Knowing What to Do* (Chattanooga, TN: Turning Point, 1997), pp. 14-15.

The *gotcha* is: Does anyone ever feel as good they look? I doubt it. I have this theological conviction that everybody's struggling to one degree or another with something they'd rather not talk about. Making a good part of my living as an interviewer, I met only one person who persisted in claiming he wasn't struggling with anything.

His closest friends disagreed with him strongly.

I believe the friends. Sorry.

Once upon a time, I recruited a support group of high school kids with the flyer below. It wasn't a very large group, but it was one of the best I ever had. Maybe because it started where we were instead of where we were supposed to be.

This is why the war on drugs is misguided: it deals only with what's obvious. The real threat is the cancer that's not so obvious. What's really wrong? Let's take a swing at fixing that.

FOR MORE ON FINDING WHAT'S REALLY WRONG, GO TO PAGE **38** AND READ ABOUT TOXICITY.

O·U·T·O·F·C·O·N·T·R·O·L
a small group for individuals of the senior high persuasion

Everybody's got problems; you know that, right? That's what this new group is for—to help you zero in on the problems that threaten to control your life.

"Oh, I don't have any of *those* kinds of problems," you say. Well, not so fast. Do you ever find yourself doing things that surprise you—things you didn't set out to do, maybe even swore you wouldn't do? Pretty frustrating.

> Eating too much, *sleeping too much*, nail-biting, *drinking*, sexual compulsiveness, *showing off and regretting it later*, intense anger, *saying yes when you meant to say no*, saying no for no good reason, *compulsive cleaning*, unreasonable fear, *trouble sleeping*, jumping trains, *people-pleasing*, burning things, *having to be right*, driving fast, *nicotine addiction*, pimple popping (really!), *finger drumming*, gambling, *bad-mouthing*, fighting, *being "nice,"* keeping people waiting, *lying about things that don't matter*, compulsive exercise, *exaggerating*, fantasies, *breaking things*, turning everything into a joke, *perfectionism*, conformity…

Is anything in this box a problem for you?

Where these things are, there's something else going on under the surface. Could be big; might be small. Maybe you know immediately what that *other thing* is; maybe you don't. The important thing is, when you know what it is, you can do something about it. That's a fact.

This group will help you identify things that could become life-controlling problems. And once you've identified them, you'll be able to take the necessary steps to control them instead of the other way round.

How does that sound? If you think it seems like something you want to check out, join us on Tuesday night from 7-9 at Jim Hancock's house. No pressure. It's completely confidential, it's centered around the Bible, and if you come once and decide it's not for you, that's fine.

Questions? Call Jim Hancock for details.

So, if our kids are numbed out, then . . .

Our kids are in pain and, if they've learned anything in our chemotherapeutic culture, they've learned that pain is not to be endured. So they, like the generations before them, numb their pain in relationships, behaviors, and substances. But that's nuts. Numbing out works for a little while, but in the end it makes people die, or wish they could. Here's what we can do about it.

Acknowledge their pain. Kids feel discounted most of the time. A Barna Research study found eighty-four percent of thirteen- to eighteen-year-old kids believe adults think they're lazy, seventy-four percent believe adults think they're rude, seventy percent believe adults think they're sloppy.[3]

> That's gotta hurt. You can argue that's not what you think about kids but, if most kids believe that's how most adults see them, the damage is done.

The best we can do goes beyond having good relationships with the kids in our lives. I think we have to acknowledge the essential humanness of every kid and admit the world is not a particularly safe place for them.

I wrote a performance piece for high school kids. It's called *In a Perfect World*. A video version appeared in *EdgeTV*. I'm fascinated by the different responses *Perfect World* gets from kids and adults.

[3] Barna Research Group in *USA Today*, May 4, 1998, reported in *Youthworker Journal*, September/October 1998, page 19.
[4] *EdgeTV*, Edition 19, Edge Communications, Inc., Box 35005, Colorado Springs, CO 80935, 800-616-3343.

In a Perfect World

In a perfect world
Parents don't fight all the time,
Women and men are partners,
Kids matter
There's no word for disrespect
In a perfect world
What you see is what you get,
People say what they mean,
No one sneaks around,
Yes means yes,
No means no,
And Hide and Seek is just a game.
In a perfect world
Nobody needs an aspirin,
No one drinks to forget,
Food is not a drug,
There's nothing to feel bad about.
In a perfect world
There's no word for enemy,
No word for cheater,
Or liar
There's no word—
In a perfect world—
for Crazy
Sick
Broken
Wasted
In a perfect world
There's no word for stranger.
In a perfect world,
The Lion takes the Lamb to lunch,
And the Lion picks up the check.
In a perfect world
Everyone has enough.
In a perfect world
There's no word for *no*
Only yes.
Work has meaning,
Play is worship,
Desire is prayer.[4]

Many adults take *In a Perfect World* personally. They think it's angry, hostile, sarcastic, attacking. Most kids think it's wistful and hopeful—bittersweet. They know they don't live in a perfect world, but they'd like to. Kids don't tend to *blame* anybody for the imperfection. They don't seem to feel mad after they hear *Perfect World*. They seem to feel relieved that someone knows this is not the way it's supposed to be. Kids seem to think, *If we know the world is broken, we can at least stop pretending everything is fine.* At most, maybe we can try to do something to fix it.

If you think that's hopelessly naïve, maybe you should stop reading and use this book for a doorstop. Kids need to know that we know. And they can't know that unless we tell them.

Find your own feelings. I'm not the kind of Christian who can say, "Every day with Jesus is sweeter than the day before." Not anymore.

I used to be. I used to practice a form of Christianity that took me, as one wag put it, *out of sin and straight into denial*. I wanted desperately to believe the popular (if not very biblical) notion that my old life was all behind me. So I did. I believed it and said it right out loud. Meanwhile, I gained fifty pounds, created a small mountain of debt, fell into sexual compulsion, honed the fine edge of sarcasm, and learned to lie again (a skill I briefly lost when I embarked on my Christian journey, then took to a new level when I rediscovered it).

I didn't find the courage to acknowledge my daughter's pain until I acknowledged my pain. That was hard. The alternative was impossible.

Now I'm the kind of Christian who says I really need Jesus every day or I know I'll mess up. Food, money, sex, sarcasm, lying—these are ways I have numbed my pain and they became life-controlling problems for me. If, by sheer force of character, I was going to get better, I would have by now. I haven't gotten better. In many ways I'm *doing* better, but I haven't *gotten* better. That's the kind of Christian I am: a Christian who hasn't gotten better and who hopes like crazy Jesus shows up today because I don't dare try it alone.

Oddly enough, there's a certain freedom in that. If the kids in my life are struggling, and they are, I'm a relatively safe person to confide in because I'm struggling too. That admission may not do much to establish my authority but it goes a long way toward affirming my authenticity. Plus, it's the truth.

Take responsibility for your own story. By and large people don't take responsibility for their actions and subsequent consequences.

Kids know that's upside down even as they learn to do it themselves. But learn it they do. It's part of the potent, informal curriculum in our culture.

There is, however, a class of citizens who do take responsibility. They're people who got caught or just ran out of the energy it takes to keep up the pretense that everything is all right when, in fact, everything is a mess.

> **Pay no attention to the man behind the curtain! By the time we say it, it's too late, everybody knows.**

In another era, a preacher named Carlisle Barney said, "You will know the truth and the truth will make you flinch before it sets you free." Boy, did he have our number—mine, at least. Confession is good for the soul and our collective soul is in serious need of something good. Until we tell the truth to ourselves and each other and, not least of all, to our children, we're gonna have a tough time with nurture because we can't give what we ain't got.

The solution, in my humble but no doubt accurate opinion, is to take responsibility for our own stories in all their grit and glory: the truth, the whole truth, nothing but the truth. I think it was Garrison Keillor who concluded that, sooner or later, our children will find out the truth about us. It's inevitable.

So autobiographies are our chance to set the record straight before they start nosing around the attic. And don't bother lying. That will only make things worse when they find out the truth, which they will. And who wants to have the kids, now in their fifties, rooting around the family plot, exhuming the body in the dead of night, moving it to an unmarked grave on the edge of the cemetery? For the kids' sake, write your autobiography.

Better yet, speak it to them directly. I'm not suggesting an airing of all the dirty laundry in your hamper. Not necessarily. If you think it's going to be a shock to the children (because you've kept silent too long), start by admitting you have a hamper. If nobody dies, describe the general nature of your private stains one at a time, as appropriate. Each time you open the hamper, note whether anybody dies. If not, be on the lookout for the next time something in the basket might help your child with *his* dirty laundry.

5 Ernest Hemingway, *A Farewell to Arms* (New York: Scribner, 1957), p. 249.

Enough with the metaphor. Just tell your own stories. Don't be inappropriate. Don't make other people feel worse so you can feel better. Don't tell your stories on Christmas Eve and then add, "Oh, and by the way, I'm leaving." Pull that stunt and you'll never make it to the family plot to begin with.

But still, dig deep, swallow hard, tell your stories. I am. I believe it's working.

And just in case you think I mean you oughta tell about all the bad stuff you've ever done, you're only partly right. I also mean all the bad stuff that was done to you. Don't be petty; that's the easy stuff. Go for the real stuff, the stuff behind your stuff. Were you abused as a child? Don't answer too quickly; think about it. Were you abused? Degraded? Diminished? Marginalized? Hurt? If yes, then say it. Did you grieve? Say it. Without trivializing the experience or disowning yourself, talk about your grief. Don't wallow, tell. Talk. Trust. Feel. If you can't, stop pretending to be an adult and ask for help.

Is that too harsh? Because I want you to know I'm talking to me, and you just happen to be listening in. I now know no one gets off easy. Hemingway nailed it:

The world breaks everyone, and afterward many are strong at the broken places.[5]

Then he put a gun in his mouth and blew away that magnificent brain. Proving, perhaps, that knowing is not enough. Living is a do-or-die proposition.

Teach healthy self-assessment. Self-assessment is the art of figuring out where I'm at in the moment. It's global positioning for the emotions. There are three coordinates:

- How am I doing physically?
- How am I doing emotionally?
- How are my relationships?

In a moment, we'll look at the vocabulary that drives self-assessment but first, this short cut: Somebody in the short, illustrious history of Alcoholics Anonymous—God bless A.A.: Get that many screwups in one room and they're gonna figure out a whole bunch about what went wrong—someone came up with an acronym that describes when recovering addicts are most likely to slip. The acronym is HALT.

Don't let yourself get too:

Hungry

Angry

Lonely

Tired

This marvelously simple tool has gotten me out of more binds than I can recount. A couple of weeks ago I was ready to have it out with everybody in the company. Things were not going as anybody planned. In fact, it was as if nobody had planned at all, which wasn't true, so I was really angry. So angry, in fact, that I paused outside the door I was about to break down. I HALTed out there and asked myself:

- *Am I hungry?* Uh, yeh. I ate about six or seven hours ago. My blood sugar is subterranean.
- *Who am I angry with and why?* Actually, my anger has very little to do with the people behind this door. I'm angry with someone in another room who agreed to one thing then did another, and left me holding the bag.
- *Am I lonely?* Yep. I feel totally isolated right now.
- *Am I tired?* Yesterday was very long, last night very short.

All that took about five seconds. I turned around and went to my office, ate a PowerBar, called my wife to chat for a few minutes, thought about what I really wanted to say to the person who bailed on the agreement, and looked at my to-do list to see what could be postponed for a fresh start tomorrow.

That done, I had a brief but pointed discussion with the one I was really mad at, finished a couple of details, turned off the lights, and went home. Much healthier than the drive-by shooting I nearly executed on the rest of the team.

I've seen HALT work for kids, too—never more dramatically than for my friend Brian. When we talked about HALT, a light came on for Brian. He described his afternoon routine: Finish school, drive to work, consume Kit Kats and twenty ounces of Mountain Dew, clock in, and go to work.

"And what happens about thirty minutes after that?" I asked.

"I crash," he said thoughtfully. "I get cranky and I'm not fit to work with."

"What do you think you could do differently?"

"I could eat smarter," he said, and did—the next day and every day since (more or less). And it changed his life. No kidding. It changed his life the way learning to type changes people's lives. It's not the gift of speech, but it's a potent new tool, a shortcut, a way to improve the utility of the gift.

My modest proposal: Learn to HALT, then teach it to your children. Better yet, learn it together.

Teach a sophisticated emotional vocabulary.
Modern kids suffer from language inflation. They inherited an impoverished emotional vocabulary and their verbal sophistication is that of a four-year-old fixated on poopy language. Listen to kids when they're not aware you're there—I mean nice, middle-class, white children, not rich snots or poor street waifs. Listening to ordinary kids shoot the breeze is like watching the Smurfs on television. If you haven't had the pleasure, let me run it down for you. *Smurf*, the noun, means a small blue person who does inane things to the delight of small children, we don't know why. But *smurf* is also a troubling and meaningless adjective, a word that modifies every other *smurfing* sentence. Do you see what I'm getting at? The English language is *smurfed* up beyond all recognition. I'm not kidding. And we have no idea what the *smurf* it means.

I don't want any Smurfs mad at me. I'm not saying they're bad blue people. I'm just using their manner of speaking as an example. It's not like I'm telling them to go *smurf* themselves. I imagine they're already *smurfed* by definition. I could be wrong.

I don't think we can understand the generations behind us without assessing the impact of language inflation. Sex, violence, drunkenness, failure, insult, enthusiasm, excellence, pain— one word says it all and the word rhymes with buck, cluck, duck, muck, and stuck. It's the most extreme word in the English language and it doesn't mean anything. Never has one word covered so much ground and said so little.

Consequently, there is no language for outrage. If a person regularly uses our most extreme language in ordinary discourse with his best friends, what then? There's nothing left for his enemies. In the absence of language what's left but to act it out? He'd really *better* have a gun under the seat of his car, hadn't he?

This is a knotty problem. And, like every knotty problem, we dare not overlook it or it will certainly be there the next time we look—and the next.

I'm all for establishing blame wherever possible. When I was a boy, I believe I understood sailors were the cause of this problem. Later, I think I recall hearing the indelicacy had been hijacked by truckers. Most recently, if I'm not mistaken, truckers offloaded the blame on the entertainment industry's dock and there it sits for the moment. So, for the record: I'm plenty mad at those guys and I'm gonna see to it they never work in this town again. They should know better. What were they, raised by sailors?

Don't you wish it were as simple as that?

It's not. It's as simple as this: We can teach kids a more sophisticated emotional vocabulary and help them learn to use it properly. We can teach them the difference between disappointment and frustration, surprise and shock, relief and satisfaction. It's within our power.

I grew up with binary emotions. I was on or I was off, shut down or wide open. If I laughed, I brayed like a donkey. If I cried, I went to my room overcome by shame so deep I didn't want to come out again. For me there was no chuckling, just hysteria. And there was no disappointment, only devastation. Consequently, I learned to stuff and withhold my emotions so as not to be a spectacle. And I did it for years. The first time I lost control with Susan, I laughed so hysterically that she was frightened and poured a glass of water over my head. I'm glad she didn't show me the door.

It was another fifteen years before I developed a healthy emotional vocabulary. The cheat sheet that follows was scavenged together over the years. It's not complete and many of the words are too sophisticated for young children. But it's gotten me through some difficult conversations. Sometimes I hand the list to kids and ask them to find the word that best describes what they're feeling. Sometimes I use it like a street map: Are they closer to City Hall or Washington Park; First or Fifty-Seventh?

Me: Would you say you feel more betrayed or more let down?

Kid: Uh, more let down, I guess.

Me: Well, is it closer to let down or victimized?

Kid: No, it's more let down.

Me: Let down or disrespected.

Kid: Yeh, that's what I really feel. I feel disrespected.

Me: Can you tell me about that?

Kid: He thinks his time is more valuable than mine. It's infuriating!

And we're off to the races!

Feelings, Nothing More Than Feelings . . .

Happy	
Accepted	Obnoxious
Appreciated	Optimistic
Approved of	Overjoyed
Blissful	Peaceful
Calm	Playful
Capable	Pleased
Carefree	Rapturous
Cheerful	Satisfied
Comfortable	Secure
Confident	Serene
Content	Significant
Delighted	Spirited
Ecstatic	Sunny
Elated	Thankful
Encouraged	Thrilled
Enthusiastic	Tranquil
Exhilarated	Understood
Exultant	Warm
Giddy	Welcome
Glad	
Gleeful	**Unhappy**
Grateful	Bored
High	Bothered
Hilarious	Cheerless
Hopeful	Choked Up
Hugged	Cloudy
Inspired	Dark
Jolly	Dejected
Joyous	Depressed
Knocked out	Despondent
Light	Disappointed
Lighthearted	Discontent
Like a contributor	Discouraged
Listened to	Disheartened
Lively	Distracted
Loved	Downcast
Merry	Downhearted
Mirthful	Dreadful
Needed	Dreary
	Dull

Gloomy
Glum
Held captive
Insignificant
Joyless
Melancholy
Moody
Mopey
Mournful
Oppressed
Out of sorts
Quiet
Sad
Somber
Sorrowful
Spiritless
Sulky
Sullen
Upset
Vacant
Woeful

Angry
Annoyed
Belligerent
Bent out of shape
Bitter
Boiling
Bugged
Contemptuous
Defiant
Disgusted
Enraged
Exasperated
Fuming
Furious
Incensed
Indignant
Inflamed
Infuriated
Irate
Irritated
Mad
Outraged
Peeved
Perturbed

Riled
Seething
Ticked off
Touchy
Up in arms
Worked up
Wrathful

Hurt
Abandoned
Accused
Aching
Afflicted
Agonized
Beat up
Belittled
Betrayed
Defensive
Degraded
Deprived
Diminished
Discounted
Disrespected
Grieved
Hampered
Infuriated
Injured
In Pain
Knifed in the back
Left out
Let down
Misused
Offended
Pathetic
Persecuted
Provoked
Put down
Rejected
Resentful
Scorned
Shamed
Taken advantage of
Tortured
Unappreciated
Unimportant
Unloved

Untrusted
Used
Victimized
Woeful
Worried

Frustrated
Astounded
Beat
Bewildered
Blah
Blown away
Broken
Burned out
Cold
Confused
Crushed
Deflated
Demotivated
Disoriented
Dull
Dumbfounded
Empty
Exhausted
Flat
Floored
Fried
Grief-stricken
Heartbroken
Helpless
Hollow
Humble
Humiliated
In despair
Inconsolable
Insecure
Like dying
Like giving up
Like I'm drowning
Like quitting
Like running away
Low
Lost
Miserable
Mortified
Mournful
Nauseated

Numb
Over my head
Overwhelmed
Panicky
Paralyzed
Pessimistic
Plagued
Powerless
Shamed
Shook
Shut down
Sick
Staggered
Stumped
Stunned
Tired
Weary
Worn out

Excited
Fearless
Bold
Brave
Calm
Certain
Confident
Determined
Firm
Hungry
Impatient
Invincible
Resolved
Self-reliant
Sexy
Strong

Anxious
Absorbed
Agitated
Alone
Apprehensive
Cautious
Concerned
Curious
Dependent
Distant
Distressed

Distrustful
Doubtful
Eager
Engrossed
Fascinated
Hesitant
Indecisive
Inquisitive
Intent
Interested
Intrigued
Itchy
Nosey
Perplexed
Questioning
Skeptical
Snoopy
Suspicious
Unbelieving
Uncertain
Uneasy
Uptight
Wavering

Afraid
Aghast
Alarmed
Appalled
Apprehensive
Awed
Cautious
Chicken
Cowardly
Dismayed
Fainthearted
Fearful
Fidgety
Frightened
Hesitant
Horrified
Hysterical
Immobilized
Insecure
Lonely
Nervous
Panicky

Paralyzed
Petrified
Restless
Scared
Shaky
Sheepish
Suspicious
Terrified
Threatened
Timid
Trembly

Guilty
Ashamed
Bad
Dumb
Embarrassed
Foolish
Incompetent
Infantile
Like a failure
Like a fool
Naive
Remorseful
Repentant
Ridiculous
Self-conscious
Selfish
Silly
Slow
Sorry
Stupid
Unfit
Useless
Weird
Worthless
Wrong

Sympathetic
Compassionate
Concerned
Connected
Empathetic
Moved
Understanding

Then, listen. Once you start telling your own stories the room will become safe for other people to tell their stories. That's how it works, trust me. Where do people get the courage to jump off the high dive? From the people who went before them. When the business seems risky, someone has to go first. It's a law of human nature. When you start telling your story, you're an emotional bungee jumper. *Watch this*, you say, and they do, wondering if you'll go splat when you get to the bottom. But, miraculously, you don't. You reach the end of your rope, then slowly, almost gracefully re-ascend. It's a wonderful thing. They say, *Do it again!* So you do. Not for the thrill but because you want them to know it's safe.

Sooner or later a loved one says, *I'm ready*, and off she goes, screaming bloody murder as the ground rushes to meet her and she knows beyond all doubt you were lying, but then, just like you, she doesn't die. She reaches the end of her rope, which stretches but doesn't break, and she, too, re-ascends and knows, later if not just yet, it was worth the risk.

Here's the thing: If she says *I'm ready*, and jumps, you'd better be watching. That means you'd better listen when she tells her first story and every one she cares to risk thereafter. Otherwise you were just showing off and she'll know it and she'll despise you for it (and I'm not kidding).

You may not be able to do a thing about it, but please listen to the story. Listening may be all that's possible—and all that's required.

> Listening is different from discussing, debriefing, or giving advice. I like the term "mirroring"— when all you do is reflect back what you hear the person saying. —Alice

> Listening is not always the same as *hearing*. —Kate

One reason I'm a Christian is that Christians are such a messy lot—the Christians in the Bible certainly are a mess, though I get the impression that modern American Christians would like us to believe Jesus saves a better class of people these days. I like those old Christians. They said things like, "If we claim that we're free of sin, we're only fooling ourselves. A claim like that is errant nonsense," and, "Confess your sins to each other and pray for each other so that you can live together whole and healed."[6]

I can get behind that. If those people listened carefully enough to pray for each other, they were really listening. I mean, maybe I'm reading too much into this, but wouldn't it be impolite to pray in generalities if the guy who confessed was sitting right next to you?

> And Jesus, please help Jacob with whatever it was he was talking about there a minute ago when I was thinking about dinner. I missed the details but I know it must be a pretty big deal because he sure was crying a lot.

Jacob and I wanna hang out with people who hang on our every word, leaning forward in their chairs, chins bobbing, eyes watering because

[6] *The Message* New Testament, (Colorado Springs: NavPress, 1994), pp. 501 and 485.

they've been where we are—maybe not in the details, but they've been where we are in our hearts. That's who Jacob wants to be with and it's who I want to be with and it's who I want to *be*, for my daughter and my wife and my friends. And I can be that guy because all it is, is listening with my whole body, my whole heart, my whole self. I can do that. God help me, I can do that.

What's the most significant thing you read or thought about in this chapter?

Why do you think that's so significant?

What do you think you might want to do about that?

Don't take my word for it. What did you read here that's worth checking with a kid?

Feeling Worthless

3.7

Though they may fantasize to the contrary, lots of kids doubt anyone would miss them if they were gone.

FOR MORE ABOUT NUMBING OUT, GO TO PAGE 132.

Proposition A: Kids long for a sense of their significance.

Proposition B: If they don't get it from the ones they love, they'll love the ones from whom they get it.

If you sunk out of sight, would you leave a ripple? Would the world be worse off without you? A great many kids can't offer a convincing *Yes!* to that question. They don't believe they hold any particular place in the order of things; they don't believe they contribute anything concrete. Though they may fantasize to the contrary, lots of kids doubt anyone would miss them if they were gone.

I can totally relate to this. I question these things and I'm twenty-three years old.
—Alice

Just to be sure we're on the same page: That's a *bad* feeling. Feeling insignificant drives kids to great lengths—sometimes right off the cliff.

Some kids go to extremes in search of significance. Academics, sports, business, the arts . . . all these carry the cultural seal of approval and, unfortunately, they can swallow every ounce of a kid's energy. Don't yell at me. I'm not saying these are bad things. I'm saying they don't create significance. Many people who excel at these enterprises find the only thing they need at the end of the day is a little more—just enough more to numb the pain of not feeling O.K.

If, for some reason, nothing on the A List works, there are other measures of significance: sexual prowess, bacchanalian drug use, fighting, drinking, driving fast, adrenaline rushing, sale and distribution of drugs (some argue this is business), gun play, breaking and entering . . . These, too, offer a measure of fame and significance.

Again, just to be sure we're on the same page: If you think these things happen mainly among urban youth, it's time to buy a newspaper.

Of course some kids settle for small significance. Some kids search for significance in the mirror and do whatever's necessary to get an approving look. A few die trying. Some kids look for significance in the eyes of one other person and give themselves wholly when they believe they've found "the one." Some cease believing in significance. They just wanna look significant.

These kids are simultaneously proud and afraid. An impoverished fifteen-year-old told me, "I steal because I have to look proper." He lived with his mother and siblings in a broken car on the streets of Los Angeles. What can I say? Image is everything. You are what you own. It's not whether you win or lose, it's how you look playing the game. No doubt, he looked good.

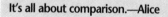

Image is nothing/Image is everything. Very confusing.—Eli

It's all about comparison.—Alice

That's where conspicuous consumption comes from. Remember conspicuous consumption? Someone defined it as buying things we don't need with money we don't have to impress people we don't like. It's the conviction that significance comes from looking right.

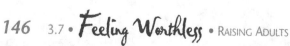
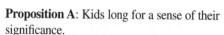

"Never Let 'Em See You Sweat" is the first and greatest commandment. And the second is like unto it: "Be Cool." If being cool and being honest are hard to do at the same time, and if human significance depends on being cool, honesty will have to wait. Sorry.

> Just another example of wanting to feel like other people look . . .

And why this search for significance? Maybe because kids aren't allowed to contribute in meaningful ways. Maybe because everything in the culture tells them to wait until they grow up—but don't wait too long. Maybe because we convince them they are what they *own*, they are how they *look*, they are what they *do*.

So, if our kids feel worthless then . . .

Ours are the first eyes into which our kids look for signs of recognition. Here's what we can do:

Encourage perceptions of personal value. Kids need to learn they are valuable apart from what they do. They won't just know it. Any parent who finds himself tempted to say the words, "Hey, you know I love you!" might do well to ask himself, "If he knows I love him, why am I working so hard to sell it right now?"

> This isn't gonna be easy. Look at how we meet new people: "Hey, I'm Frank." "Wuhl, glad ta meetcha, Frank. Whadaya do?" What do I do? About what? We don't do any better with kids: "Hey, I'm Franky." "Wuhl, glad ta meetcha, Franky... Uh... Whadaya wanna do when you grow up?" We gotta come up with better questions.

If you want to raise someone who is a human *being* and not a human *doing*, separate what she does from who she is. Feel free to disagree with me here, but I've chosen not to use the words, "I'm proud of you." I tell my daughter how impressed I am. I tell her how much I admire her. I don't say I'm proud of her. Here's why.

I'm afraid if I tell my daughter I'm proud of her it will sound like I had something to do with her success. I didn't. She waded out of a decent gene pool. She grew up in a home with people who love her and who nurtured her as well as we were able given a long history of craziness. She went to school in relatively affluent school districts. Beyond that context, Kate's achievement is all her own. She's blessed with a good brain operating system that she learned to use effectively. She doesn't accept easy answers and she's not an intellectual snob. She learned to articulate her thoughts directly and generously. She learned to listen well and distinguish between important information and factoids without needing to ask, "Will this be on the test?" She built a strong work ethic and a whatever-it-takes attitude. She also learned how to have fun. She knows how to listen to her friends and figure out which are *fuelers* and which are *drainers*. In the process she learned to be a fueler and how to *get* fuel when she's drained. Her skill as an actor is equal parts genius and hard work. The genius, for which she takes no credit, is an unusual ability to memorize dialog quickly. But it's hard work that turns those words into characters who are real to an audience.

I'm impressed out of my mind by all that. I'm so fortunate to know her. I admire her work and her character. But I wouldn't say I'm proud of her because those achievements are hers and hers alone.

If you think I'm just playing with words, I can only say I don't play with words—not when I'm talking about something as important as this.

Not to press my luck but I'm feeling curmudgeonly, so I think I'll take this a step further: I don't think adults should praise children.

Praise is usually related to an attribute for which the child can take no credit. Blond, straight hair, for example. Blue eyes. Ample breasts, a small waist . . . Bingo! Miss Minnesota! Talk about using up all fifteen minutes at once . . . This kind of praise is a setup. Miss Minnesota will be sorely tempted to do whatever it takes for as long as it takes to maintain the illusion that she's still seventeen and above the law of gravity.

> Or take the kid who's been praised because he's smart. "You're so smart, Buster! I'm so proud of you! Lookee here, Aunt Esther, Buster got all A's again! Buster, I'm gonna buy you the biggest ice cream sundae they make!"

Now, not only will Buster face some interesting questions around food, he'll also have to figure out which is more important in his long run: learning or getting all A's.

We know that getting A's can be accomplished by blending intellect and hard work. But it never turned out that way for Albert Einstein, who had a learning disability so severe teachers thought the boy genius was mentally retarded. Still, that doesn't mean it won't work for Buster. If, perchance, hard work plus intellect does *not* equal all A's for Buster and he's not quite up to inventing a new physics, he might reach his goal by, oh, I don't know . . . *cheating*. A lot of kids do. While I was working with kids in San Diego County, a group of A and B students approached the administration at La Jolla High School asking for a different level of academic monitoring. "We don't want to cheat," they said, "but the way things are set up, if we don't cheat it's almost impossible to keep up with people who do." I asked smart kids what they thought about that. No one disagreed.

One other option for Buster is taking easy classes. And who could blame him if the goal is getting all A's?

You see the problem? If my significance comes from how I look or what I accomplish, there will always be someone more significant than me. If not today, tomorrow. It's inevitable. I don't think any child should have to contend with that. Here's what strikes me as a better way.

Try affirmation in place of praise.
Affirmation looks at achievement and appreciates it for what it is, not what it isn't. "Wow. All A's. Way to go. Tell me how you got those grades." "Hey, good job in the play. You're very talented but that must've taken a lot of hard work. Tell me how you prepared." "May I tell you something I appreciate about you? (Duh!) I like the way you present yourself. You have an interesting sense of style. Where do you like to

FOR MORE ON PRAISE, GO TO PAGE 66.

shop? How do you choose your clothes and how you'll wear your hair?"

Affirmation expresses appreciation for accomplishment. Affirmation invites dialog.

Express unconditional love and abiding respect.

Performance-based approval isn't love. Please don't call it that. Dennis and Barbara Rainey, authors of *Parenting Today's Adolescent,* realized they'd dodged a bullet when their fourteen-year-old son's promising tennis career was sidelined by muscular dystrophy. They had separated their affirmation for Samuel's performance as an athlete from their love for him as a person. When tennis went away, Samuel was still loved.[1]

That's why language is important to me. I want to do my best to ensure that my daughter knows what I mean. Today, my love for Kate is matched by abiding respect for her. That wasn't always so. I was hard on her when she was young. I would even say that I was disrespectful toward her *because* she was young. I apologized, she forgave me, and I've been working at mending my ways for a decade. My progress is less than spectacular but clearly discernable.

Ultimately, this has to do with what clinical professionals call *locus of control.* It's a fancy way of talking about how a person is motivated. People with an internal locus of control are motivated by an inner voice—their own voice—that says, *Here's what I think, here's what I believe, here's what I value, therefore this is what I will do.*

People with an external locus of control are motivated by voices that come from outside themselves: *Here's what we expect you to do; it's what you should do.* If a kid is motivated by outside voices more than her own inner voice—don't get weird on me, this is just a metaphor—it's because her sense of significance comes from external sources. She believes she's significant only as long as others give their approval. And the approval of others is usually attached to performance more than character or *being.* Even if those voices are relatively benevolent, even if the loudest voices belong to her parents, she's in danger of believing she can't be valuable unless others tell her she's valuable.

> Here's the bind: Almost nobody thinks kids are intrinsically valuable. They don't do anything but take up space. We warehouse them in schools until they're big enough to earn some money and don't say that isn't true until we've done something *huge* to reform education in our culture.

As I write these words, the U.S. Congress is voting on a budget that could put 100,000 new teachers in public schools, 30,000 almost right away. I hope that's the next step to refocusing the classroom on students. We'll see.

Outside of youth workers, coaches, mentors and teachers, about the only adults who regularly and convincingly communicate with kids are predators (give us what we want and we'll give you candy) and retailers (you buy, therefore you are).

[1] Dennis and Barbara Rainey, with Bruce Nygren, *Parenting Today's Adolescent* (Nashville: Thomas Nelson, 1998), p. 319.

TO REVIEW AFFIRMING, AND HOW IT'S DIFFERENT FROM PRAISING, GO TO PAGE 66.

Sometimes it's hard to tell the retailers from the predators. Still, kids give them what they want. Not wholeheartedly, maybe; without joy, maybe. But they still give because maybe that's what it costs to feel significant. At least for a moment.

~·∺·~

Here's that Christian thing again. I don't mean to harp, but it really plays into my sense of what makes people valuable. I think my daughter is valuable because she's handmade by the Creator. I don't know how God did it and I can only guess why, but I've come to believe my kid bears a faint likeness to a heavenly parent. I think I do, too. And you.

If that's true, our earth-rent is being paid by the landlord and you don't need me to tell you you're valuable. Bottom line: If my kid's in a healthy relationship with her Creator, she'll have a pretty healthy sense of herself and the rest of us. So I want her to be motivated by an inner voice instead of an outside voice, even if the outside voice is mine. I think an internal locus of control is a sign of health.[2] Okay, enough of that. There's more, but this isn't the time or place for it.

Expose kids firsthand to legitimate heroes. One other thing you can do to increase your child's sense of significance is to introduce him, firsthand, to real heroes. I'm not thinking about Michael Jordan or Tipper Gore here, unless they happen to be family friends. I mean Uncle Chuck and Aunt Lu. I mean a high quality youth worker whom you know well enough to trust. I mean any decent, high-functioning, authentic adult. These are the people

who influenced my daughter. They're the ones who influenced me. Colin Powell is, no doubt, a swell role model. We just don't happen to know him. Had my daughter ever gotten close enough to be influenced by him, I'm sure it would have been good. Kate *did* get in touch with more ordinary heroes. Watching them, listening to them, testing their words against their actions, getting close enough to see their faults as well as their strengths—these are the experiences that shaped her.

🏃 What's the most significant thing you read or thought about in this chapter?

🏃 Why do you think that's so significant?

🏃 What do you think you might want to do about that?

🏃 Don't take my word for it. What did you read here that's worth checking with a kid?

[2] For more about external locus of control, go to *The Boy Who Believed in Magic: A Picture Book for Big People*, by Jim Hancock (Berkeley: Blue Sky Books, 1999).

Getting Schoolteachers to Finally Shut Up About Money: A Modest Proposal

I'm fed up with teachers and their nifty salaries! What is needed is a little perspective. Teachers should be paid babysitting wages. That's right—instead of paying outrageous taxes, I'd give them $3 an hour. And, I'm only going to pay them for five hours. That's all they work anyway. Let's see, that's $15 a day for each child. Even if a parent had more than one child, it's still cheaper than private day care.

Now, each teacher should be able to handle twenty children. That's about ten less than they have now. So, that's $15 x 20 = $300 a day. But the state requires students to attend only 180 days a year, so I'm not going to pay them for all their vacations or time away from the children. Let's see . . . $300 times 180 days is $54,000. Hmmmmmmmmmm?

I know what you teachers are thinking . . . what about ten years of experience or a master's degree? Okay, I'd pay you minimum wage instead of just babysitting wage. You'd have to read the kids a story or throw in some simple math. Minimum wage, I'd round off to $5 an hour . . . times five hours times twenty children. That's $500 a day times 180 days. That's $90,000 . . . oops!

Gee, maybe babysitting wages are too good for teachers . . .

—From Ralph Paisley on the Internet[3]

[3] mikeys-funnies@ youthspecialties.com, August, 21, 1998, original source unknown.

Transliterate

3.8

When I got my first

look at *Sesame*

Street in the Spring

of 1969, I knew

everything had

changed.

Our daughter, Kate, preparing for her first screen role, asked Susan to run lines with her. Susan was busy with something or other and, since Kate was watching *Animaniacs* on TV while she studied her lines, Susan begged off until Kate took more time to memorize. An hour later, *Animaniacs* having given way to *Rug Rats* or some such, Kate announced she was ready to run the lines. Susan chided her for dividing her attention between the script and the television. Kate replied that she was *ready*, thank you very much, and with that she handed Susan the script and proved she had memorized twenty-two pages of dialog. Susan was impressed. I was envious.

Kate grew up fluent in a new *televisual* language few adults understand. Like most (though not all) young Americans, Kate is comfortable multitasking. She takes in, processes, and makes sense of information from more than one source at a time.

I do that better than my parents and, I think, better than my slightly pre-Boomer sister. Listening to music while I write helps me focus on the task by masking other stimuli. I know a lot of people my age who do that. What interests me is that Kate uses television the same way—and that I can't do. I'm overstimulated by the pictures, my attention is divided. To Kate, TV is white noise, occupying just enough of her senses to keep her from being distracted.

Like most of her peers, Kate is capable of high-quality straight-line reasoning. She processes from premise to conclusion as well as anyone I know. But she thinks naturally in *gestalts*, drawing meaning from the whole picture even more easily than if she concentrates on elements of the picture and adds them together to get the meaning.

She does this because it's how she learned to think. People who grew up in more linear decades call kids the *MTV Generation*. In fact, they are probably more the *Sesame Street Generation*.

Did you watch *Sesame Street* with your children? I stumbled on the program when I was a junior in high school and I was floored. It all happened so fast I couldn't believe the show was a whole half-hour. The letters, the numbers, the crayon-colored sets, the music . . . and the jokes! What a feast!

Howdy Doody retired about the time I started caring and local children's programming was just killing time every afternoon. But mornings were different. In the morning, all young eyes were on CBS where The Captain was king. *Captain Kangaroo!* He was the man! I grew up watching Bunny Rabbit's ping-pong balls rain down on Mr. Green Jeans, and the Captain reading *Iron Mike* and *The Little Engine that Could* and *Curious George.* It was a golden age.

When I got my first look at *Sesame Street* in the Spring of 1969, I knew everything had changed. This was fast-moving, intense, and— meaning no disrespect to Mr. Green Jeans, Tom Terrific, Mr. Moose, or, of course, our beloved Captain—*Sesame Street* was exciting! This children's television was rocket-powered.

So, naturally, it produced rocket-powered learners. The Children's Television Workshop saw more clearly than anyone had that children have short attention spans. And they wrote to it. The bits were short and punchy. The repetition of ideas was varied. In a half-hour program, children experienced counting with claymation, a pastry chef with a stack of pies, and Bill Cosby straining hard to remember his numbers. And the show was brought to us by the letter "B" as in baseball, brick, bus, and big business.

> **Sesame Street** paved the way for MTV. No question about that. Young Americans were used to seeing a lot of images strung together in a nonlinear story line. Adults looked at music videos and thought, *I don't get it.* Kids saw the videos as little movies, processed them quickly to see if there was any take-away value (usually there wasn't), then moved on. It all fit the way they learned to think. Too bad most classroom instruction didn't—and still doesn't—fit as well.

Everything revolved again in the early eighties. I don't mean MTV. That's an extension of *Sesame Street*. The new light that dawned in the eighties glowed from the screens of personal computers.

Personal computers spread in the eighties like television in the fifties: one user at a time. Kids took to them like we took to television when we were young. And for the same reason: Computers may have been a big adjustment for us; to our children they are transparent technology.

> *Forty-one percent of 13-19 year-old Americans access the Internet at least once a month.*
> — ***Roper Starch Worldwide***[1]

And then there's e-mail. Some people hate it. Others, like me, use e-mail more than snail mail. I'm not alone. As of June 1998, America OnLine subscribers alone (something over twelve million of them) sent *225 million* "instant messages" a day compared with about 330 million first-class letters mailed by the whole population of the U.S., about 270 million souls.[2] E-mail is immediate, direct, and the rules are simpler than traditional letters. These factors combine to produce a level of communication that exceeds anything I've ever experienced. I've been especially pleased by the frequency and depth of e-mail exchanges with young friends when they go to college. There's something about the medium that makes them free to say what's on their minds and in their hearts in the moment instead of waiting until they come home for Christmas break. I like that a bunch. So much, it outweighs the small inconveniences and imprecisions that occasionally crop up. All of which is irrelevant. Kids use electronic mail as naturally as the telephone.

> *Internet users under the age of 18 will reach 77 million worldwide by 2005.*
> — ***Computer Economics***[3]

The learning tools available to our children are more immediate, more user-friendly, and more widely available than breakthrough technologies were when we were young. Sure, our generation took a giant leap forward, but our children move at light speed.

[1] cited in *Wired*, August 1999, p. 71.
[2] *Fast Company*, October 1998, p. 84.
[3] cited in *Wired*, August 1999, p. 72.

If your child were multilingual, would that be a bad thing? Well, chances are, she is. Or think of it this way. Your daughter has more than one brain operating system. It's as if her mind effortlessly reads files in *MS DOS* and *Macintosh OS* and *Linux* and *Whatever's Next!* I don't know what's not to like about this.

This is fine, except that it doesn't come so naturally for me. I have to strain to keep up with the conversation in this new language. I'm afraid I feel like . . . my father.

It can do its homework, talk on the phone, and listen to the radio all at the same time . . . And at the end of the evening it all makes sense.

—**MTV creator, Robert Pitman, on the generation that watches his programming**[4]

[This generation of kids can] speed-read visuals. They're getting an education in how dialectical montage works. In this vast commercial junkpile of record advertisement that most music video is, what's also going on is a groundbreaking work to establish a whole new kind of tele-visual language.

—**Michael Nash,** Los Angeles Times, **December 24, 1989**

Michael Nash, media arts curator at the Long Beach Museum of Art, called this other language (the one our kids understand) *dialectical montage.*

You remember Hegel's dialectic method. You don't? Well it went something like this: Two Greek gods, Thesis and Antithesis, meet. They mud wrestle until you can't tell which is which. Then they make a baby named Synthesis who grows up to resemble both Thesis and Antithesis but refuses to speak to either of them.

Dialectical montage strings together (that's *montage*) opposing ideas and images (that's *dialectic*).

That's the kind of thinking our children have learned to do (and no, it's not a communist plot). They're not thrown off when things don't seem to fit; they just keep looking for patterns. Our children don't automatically take any point of view as gospel truth. Kids doubt there's only one answer to most questions. They can be persuaded, but they won't be bullied.

If you think that's just warmed over sixties relativism, I think you're not looking close enough.

While there's a high, and in many respects admirable, degree of tolerance among modern kids, they haven't suspended judgment altogether (a claim not all of us can make for ourselves at their age). At this writing:

- Young Americans are in the vanguard of practical ecology—the president of the Sierra Club is twenty-five years old.
- The number of Peace Corps volunteers is twenty-seven percent higher today than it was a decade ago.[5]

[4] quoted by Neil Howe and Bill Strauss in *13th Gen* (New York: Vintage Books, 1993), p. 182.

[5] *Encyclopædia Britannica* 1998 and Peace Corps Web site (www.peace-corps.gov).

- The approval for casual sex among adolescents declined from fifty-two percent in 1987 to forty-two percent in 1997.[6]
- Thirty-eight percent of eighteen- to twenty-four-year-olds, and more than half of twenty-five- to thirty-three-year-olds, volunteered within the past year.[7]
- Twenty-five to thirty-four year-olds are trying to start businesses at a rate that triples the efforts of thirty-five- to fifty-five-year-olds.
- Seventy-two percent of eighteen- to twenty-four-year-olds think their generation "has an important voice." The same survey found that respondents tend to see themselves as ambitious, determined, and independent—no matter what their elders think.
- Ninety-one percent of twenty-one- to thirty-three-year-olds agreed with the statement: "If I just work hard enough, I will achieve what I want."[8]

The point is simply this. Our children aren't checked out, they aren't slackers, and they aren't stupid. But the way they think is different. As different as the way we think is from *our* parents. All because they've experienced a different set of stimuli.

If you put it that way, they're not so different at all.

So, if our kids are transliterate, then...
Chances are, the kids you care for learn differently from you. It's because their minds are patterned differently. That's not bad, it's just different. So be an encourager.

Figure out how your kid learns and encourage her in that process. If your child needs peace and quiet to learn, help her find it. If peace and quiet includes the white noise of music or television or the collaboration of a study group—and her learning bears out the methodology—don't refuse those elements to your daughter just because that's not the way you learn. And be aware that, if you have two children, each may learn differently.

It's results that count. I remember watching the exceedingly ugly tennis of Rod Laver when I was young. Tennis coaches cringed at the way he played and, except for one tiny thing, he would've been a laughing stock. The one tiny thing is he was wildly, convincingly, consistently successful. When it comes to tennis (or learning), you can't argue with that. Go ahead, show your child the "right" way to learn. But be alert for signs that will tell you how he learns best and encourage him to go with that. This is not, after all, a moral issue.

Encourage lifelong learning instead of binge-and-purge cramming. I don't know who gets credit for this line but I'm in his or her debt:

Don't let school get in the way of a good education.

Wow. I think that's really good. I think school is good too, but not at the expense of learning to learn. If you ask me, that's what school is supposed to be about—it's supposed to equip us to learn for the rest of our lives.

[6] Harpers Index, quoted in a sermon by Reverend John H. Stevens
[7] Harpers Index, quoted in a sermon by Reverend John H. Stevens.
[8] *Time*, June 9, 1997, pp. 58-68.

This is why a C can be better than an A—if the C comes from wrestling with difficult content instead of coasting through the usual stuff.

But, you protest, if my kid gets C's, she can't get into a decent college.

Sure she can. If you mean a *prestigious* college, that may be a different question. But if you mean a place where a learner is set free to really learn, most of them are pretty good these days. I mean, they'd have to be with all the advanced degrees awarded to college professors by prestigious schools these days. Right?

American colleges and universities awarded nearly half a million master's and doctor's degrees in 1995.
—**Encyclopædia Britannica**

Look, I know what I'm talking about here. I started my higher education at Florida State University in the fall of 1970. My scholastic performance was outstanding enough to merit a letter from the academic dean, who felt my 1.92 grade-point average made me a student worth keeping an eye on.

They didn't kick me out; I moved to the West Coast of my own free will. Once there, I enrolled at San Bernardino Valley College, a community college of some local distinction. The contrast between Valley College and Florida State was startling. I'm sure the teaching assistants who lectured hundreds of us at a time at FSU were very nice young people, but frankly they were no match for the Ph.D.s who taught us at SBVC. Most of my classes at the community college had fifteen to twenty students and most of my instructors had their doctorates.

I know what you're thinking: *Sure, he was in Southern California. Everybody wanted to live in Southern California in those days, even Ph.D.s.* But what you don't understand is that I was in *San Bernardino.* The armpit of the Inland Empire. Smog City. Nobody wanted to live there. San Bernardino was like one of those twenty-four-hour restaurants people end up at when everything else is closed.

Well, I ended up in an awesome learning environment and, equipped with an attitude adjustment, I did very well there. Then I transferred to the California State College at San Bernardino—*The Forgotten Cal State.* Cal State San Berdoo was so far down the food chain the only mascot left was the Coyote.

We did what we could, mainly in classes even smaller than Valley College (fifteen was pretty big at Cal State San Bernardino). And the percentage of Ph.D.s in the classroom was, of course, higher still. And they were tough and they were hands-on and I finished college with a 3.85 cumulative GPA, a working knowledge of my field, and the skills to think and learn for the rest of my life. Go Coyotes!

Maybe you're thinking this just proves your point. Fine. Close the book and mail it to me. I'll give your money back, or mow your lawn, or something. But I'll tell you this. Nobody at my no-name schools took tests for anybody else. My professors knew every one of us by name and they knew our writing styles well enough that buying term papers was out of the question. I'll tell you one other thing. I've been working with kids for a long time and my spies have been everywhere in the House of Learning. One thing that holds true is that the learners learn, wherever they are. And the kids whose most burning question is "Will this be on the test?" don't even know what they don't know.

Eric Hoffer said, "In times of change, learners inherit the earth, while the learned find themselves beautifully equipped to deal with a world that no longer exists."[9] In a changing economy, who can afford to depend on others to complete their education? Help your child become a learner for life.

Learn from your kid. See what you can learn from your kid. Math? Computers? The Web? Speed reading? Ecology? If your kid knows it better than you, she'll learn even more when she becomes your teacher.

What's the most significant thing you read or thought about in this chapter?

Why do you think that's so significant?

What do you think you might want to do about that?

Don't take my word for it. What did you read here that's worth checking with a kid?

[9] quoted by H. Stephen Glenn and Jane Nelsen in *Raising Self-Reliant Children in a Self-Indulgent World* (Rocklin, CA: Prima Publishing/St. Martins Press, 1989), dedication page.

Spiritually Hungry

3.9

Truth be told, most kids would prefer to satisfy their spiritual hunger at a smorgasbord.

Kids aren't inclined to accept—or, for that matter, *reject*—religious notions just because they are widely accepted or traditional. In practical terms, nothing is particularly traditional for most kids—most haven't spent much time at church.

But kids think about spiritual things a lot. And they're wide open. This may surprise you. But maybe not. Why would they be different from us?

They're no more nuts about having their freedom curtailed than we are, but they have an appetite for what's transcendent in the world. Truth be told, most kids would prefer to satisfy their spiritual hunger at a smorgasbord—which is exactly what we have in our culture.

William Bennett, Julia Cameron, Jack Canfield, Stephen Carter, Laurie Beth Jones, Anne Lamott, John Paul II, Laura Schlesinger—all are writing best-sellers out of spiritual conviction. They're all good Americans (except the Pope, who's a good citizen of the world) so they would probably tend to tolerate each other. But they vary widely on the details of their convictions. Each has something pretty specific in mind and it's not just "It-doesn't-matter-what-you-believe-as-long-as-you-believe-something."

> **Right. If it doesn't matter what I believe as long as I believe something, I *believe* I'll have another beer.**

Pop music is as full of God-talk at the turn of the century as it was in 1972, at the height of the Jesus Movement. The *Wall Street Journal* made much of the fact that, once *Soundscan* was in place to track actual sales, it turns out Contemporary Christian Music holds a bigger market share than jazz or classical music. For better or worse, it's certainly different.

Ouija boards are selling big again, new-agey crystals are fixtures around adolescent throats, fantasy and role-playing computer games feature mystical characters and elements. Hollywood movies and television fuel the fire. *Xena, the Warrior Princess, The New Adventures of Hercules,* and *The X-Files* draw strong audiences in syndication and seem likely to do so in perpetuity. It may be a fad, it may be a trend; whatever it is, mystery and transcendence are everywhere.

MTV ran a segment for a while in which Douglas Coupland read from his book, *Life After God.*

> *Ours was a life lived in paradise and thus it rendered any discussion of transcendental ideas pointless . . .*
>
> *Life was charmed but without politics or religion. It was the life of children of the children of the pioneers—life after God—a life of earthly salvation on the edge of heaven. Perhaps this was the finest thing to which we may aspire, the life of peace, the blurring between dream life and real life—and yet I find myself speaking these words with a sense of doubt. I think there was a trade-off somewhere along the line. I think the price we paid for our golden life was the inability to fully believe in love; instead we gained an irony that scorched everything it touched. And I wonder if this irony is the price we paid for the loss of God.*
>
> *But then I must remind myself we are living creatures—we have religious impulses—we must—and yet into what cracks do these impulses flow in a world without religion? It is something I think about every day. Sometimes I think it is the only thing I should be thinking about.*[1]

[1] Douglas Coupland, *Life After God* (New York: Pocket Books, 1994), pp. 273-274.

Once we get past the surface, this is where our children live. It's their biggest question.

When I interview adolescents on subjects like body image, lying, success, death—most any subject, really—near the end of the conversation I ask, "Where's God in all this?" Most kids have pretty well-formed answers. They may not be *sophisticated* answers; their religious experience is not very sophisticated. But they are usually well-considered answers. It may be the first time an adult has asked them to talk about it, but this is not the first time the question crossed their minds.

It's this absence of spiritual interaction with adults that surprises me. Most kids don't have genuine *God* conversations with adults. It's yet another thing they learn from other kids on the playground or at the food court. And their peers know as much about the depths of the human spirit as they know about the depths of human sexual intimacy.

God is so ambiguous.—Eli

At this point, God is hard to believe in, but I'm working on that.—Ben

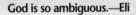

As far as kids know, all religions are pretty much the same. Now that I think about it, that's an opinion shared by a lot of us. Maybe that's why we don't talk with kids about spirituality: We don't know anything either.

What's interesting to me is that kids have been asking these questions all along. A lot of us thought life without God seemed like a good idea; now we're not so sure. I don't think our children ever were.

> It is something I think about every day. Sometimes I think it is the only thing I should be thinking about.
> —*Douglas Coupland*

So, if our kids are spiritually hungry, then . . .

Kids know there must be a place for their spiritual impulses to flow and they don't understand when people pretend they don't have any.

Consider your own spiritual impulses. Unless you have an honest stake in keeping your distance from God, why not revisit what you believe—and *why*—as part of helping your children grow. If your biggest beef with intentional spirituality has more to do with your parents than with the Creator, reconsider the Creator apart from your parents. This is not about childish stories or hypocrites in the church. It's about whether being a whole human being includes your spirit.

From time to time, I retrace my spiritual path, going back to the beginning as well as I can, searching for footprints along the way. Usually, it's an exercise in remembering what happened and why. This year, that took the form of an essay for a book called *What's Your Story?*[2]

Whatever else happens, the process keeps me honest. (Some might say, *No, it only deepens the lie.* Be that as it may, if they're right, it's a pretty good lie that makes a genuinely better man.) Every time through, I see where I stumbled on the path, where I slipped, fell, crawled, struggled back to my feet or was lifted, carried along for a while, then set back on solid footing. I'm not saying it's fun. I'm saying it's useful. In this realm, as in every other:

[2] Toben and Joanne Heim, *What's Your Story?* (Colorado Springs: Piñon Press, 1999).

Growth is the only evidence of life.

—JOHN HENRY NEWMAN[3]

Open a spiritual dialog. As you get in touch with your spiritual story, tell it to your children. If you need to go find your story, that's fine. Say so. Who knows, your child may be able to help you. You don't have to be right as much as *real*. I think if you're real, sooner or later, *right* will look after itself.

Expose kids to spiritual people. Some folks will think this suggestion is far too open-ended—that you should examine the theological content of people's lives before exposing them to your children. Call me crazy but I'm not too worried about that. "Right" really does have a way of looking out for itself. Maybe not as quickly as we high-control folks would prefer, but in good time.

Lemme slice a little closer to the bone: If God is more than make-believe, God will look after the Truth. Nobody should violate her conscience on this. I'm only saying we have little to fear from honest, searching, spiritual people.

Read a book. Maybe you already have your own reading list. My favorite spiritual books (so far), alphabetized by title . . .

[3] From *Apologia Pro Vita Sua* (1864), quoted by Laurence J. Peter in *Peter's Quotations* (New York: Bantam, 1977), p. 30.

- *Addiction and Grace,* Gerald May (nonfiction, HarperCollins, 1988). A book about what's wrong, and the hope it can be made right.
- *Alcoholics Anonymous: "Big Book,"* Unknown (nonfiction, A.A. World Services, 1939). The essential manual for people who know how upside down things can get and first steps to putting things right.
- *A Prayer for Owen Meany,* John Irving (novel, William Morrow, 1989). A story about what the least likely people can do when God gets involved.
- *The Artists Way: A Spiritual Path to Higher Creativity,* Julia Cameron (lessons, Tarcher/Putnam, 1992). A personalized journey of reflection, self-knowledge, and creative decision-making.
- *The Best Christmas Pageant Ever,* Barbara Robinson (story, Avon, 1972). A funny story about why the story of Christ is really good news.
- *Bold Love,* Dan Allender and Tremper Longman, III (nonfiction, NavPress, 1992). What to do about what's wrong in relationships.
- *The Bonfire of the Vanities,* Tom Wolfe (novel, Farrar, Straus, Giroux, 1987). A story about what's wrong with everybody I ever met, starting with me.
- *Dogmatics in Outline,* Karl Barth (lectures, Harper & Row, 1959). A plain description of Christian faith from one of the smartest people in the twentieth century.
- *The Great Divorce,* C. S. Lewis (novel, Macmillan, 1946). Why people decide to believe—or not.
- *The Holy Bible: New International Version* (Bible, International Bible Society/Zondervan, 1973). A modern translation even I understand.
- *Holy the Firm,* Annie Dillard (memoir,

Harper & Row, 1977). Two years of the hard stuff.

- *The Jesus I Never Knew,* Philip Yancey (nonfiction, Zondervan, 1995). The Jesus I'm coming to know.
- *The Knowledge of the Holy,* A. W. Tozer (nonfiction, Harper & Row, 1961). A long, easy look at what sort of person God is.
- *Let's Quit Fighting About the Holy Spirit,* Peter Gilquist (nonfiction, Zondervan, 1974). How God does what God wishes and why to get out of the way.
- *Living Prayer,* Robert G. Benson (nonfiction, Tarcher, 1998). A beautifully crafted reflection on living a reflective life.
- *Mere Christianity,* C. S. Lewis (nonfiction, Macmillan, 1943). A plain description of Christian faith, first broadcast on BBC radio.
- *The Message,* Eugene Peterson (Bible, NavPress, 1994). A contemporary rendering of the New Testament that knocks my socks off.
- *Operating Instructions,* Anne Lamott (memoir, Pantheon, 1993). A memoir about how God loves us just the way we are and far too much to leave us that way.
- *Orthodoxy,* G. K. Chesterton (nonfiction, Ignatius, 1908). An intelligent defense of Christian faith that rocked the intellectual world.
- *The Practice of the Presence of God,* Brother Lawrence (letters, Spire Books, 1958). Reflections about earthshaking intimacy with God.
- *The River Why,* David James Duncan (novel, Sierra Club Books, 1983). As good an extended metaphor as I ever hope to read.
- *The Screwtape Letters,* C. S. Lewis (parody, Macmillan, 1941). A training course for demons on how to tempt humans.
- *Teaching a Stone to Talk,* Annie Dillard (essays, HarperCollins, 1982). The good, the bad, the ugly, all under the care of God.
- *Telling Secrets,* Frederick Buechner (autobiography, HarperCollins, 1991). How one man started coming clean.
- *Telling the Truth: The Gospel as Tragedy, Comedy & Fairy Tale,* Frederick Buechner (lectures, Harper & Row, 1977). How God comes in the middle of life as we know it.
- *Traveling Mercies*, Anne Lamott (essays, Pantheon, 1999). Some thoughts on faith.
- *The Trivialization of God,* Donald McCullough (nonfiction, NavPress, 1995). Exploding the illusion of a manageable deity.
- *The 24-Hour Christian,* Earl Palmer (nonfiction, InterVarsity Press, 1987). Why being a Christian depends more on God than me.
- *Word by Word: Anne Lamott's Online Diary,* Anne Lamott (memoir, www.salon magazine.com). How a talented, weird, unstable person experiences God day-to-day.

I'm not saying these are the greatest spiritual books of all time; I don't even recommend everything in them. They're on my list because they either rocked my world or put into words what I would've said if I could. I keep these books where I can easily get my hands on them.

Don't give up. I have a friend who grew up without religion. Her parents didn't give her any reason to value one sort of religion more than another. So, when she felt spiritually hungry, she took a salad bar approach, looking for something nourishing. She sampled this and that and found herself saying, *Well, that wasn't it.* About twenty years ago, after a final snack at the Self-Realization Fellowship, she found the meal she was hungry for at a little Presbyterian church. She wasn't even sure what a Presbyterian was.

Another friend led self-help seminars for as long as she could stand it. She quit, finally, because she couldn't justify selling solutions that didn't work in her own life. (Should somebody in emotional, relational, and spiritual bankruptcy take money for telling other people how to live?) The money was still there but she felt like a whore. So she gave up the money and started searching for more workable answers. To her surprise, she found a home with a group of Christians who, admittedly, had a lot more questions than answers. But the few answers they held onto seemed to be saving their souls.

I know another guy who woke up one morning to the realization he spent his days not doing drugs and his nights wondering if it was worth it. He was sober, but he was sad. So he did what 12-Steppers do when they feel stuck: He went back to the beginning. He had a breakthrough at Step Three — *We decided to turn our will and our life over to God as we understood him.* He realized, though he'd gone to church for years, he didn't understand God at all. So he embarked on a quest to find the name of his Higher Power. As it turned out, it was a name he recognized, but the Jesus he came to believe in bore little resemblance to the Sunday school Jesus of his childhood.

If you think you detect a bias in these stories, I can only say, *not on purpose.* Unless the bias is toward people whose lives were and are as messy as mine was and is. We are finding, in the God of Jesus Christ, a constant and compelling force for change. But we didn't find that force without ruling out a whole lot of other possibilities along the way. Self-improvement failed us. That's when we started doing serious business with the God of weak people.

If that's not the kind of Christian you're used to earing about, I can only guess you are listening to the wrong kind of Christian and I can only hope you'll ignore all the moralizing and nagging going on in the name of Jesus and go looking for people who are so screwed up they hardly have a right to say anything at all. It turns out these are the people who have the most to say about what it means to need a savior, and what it means to find one.

) What's the most significant thing you read or thought about in this chapter?

) Why do you think that's so significant?

) What do you think you might want to do about that?

) Don't take my word for it. What did you read here that's worth checking with a kid?

Mostly Normal

3.10

Human beings tend

to grow into adults

sooner or later, by

hook or by crook.

That's the testimony

of time.

The B^2 *Chronicles* (that's B squared as in **B**eavis and **B**utt-Head) remind us how we acted when we were young:

Hey, the B^2 Generation is going to survive just like we survived. And don't tell me you were never Beavis or Butt-Head because I know better. I was. Everybody I know was. Some of us evolved sooner and some evolved better because we got help from some unexpected sources.[1]

I take strong exception to this characterization! I don't have any idea what the man is talking about and that's the story I'm going with. I got along perfectly well with the generation ahead of me and always felt they understood me completely. Oh, there were double takes at the family reunion when my hair crept onto my shoulders. And perhaps *spirited* is not too strong a word to describe our discussions about Vietnam. And, yes, I suppose the corduroy bell bottoms and turtleneck sweater I wore to my wedding raised a few eyebrows, but do I have to remind anyone it was MY wedding! I think not. Anyway, that's about it. Unless you insist on making a big deal about the—what is the word? OUTRAGE?—my mother expressed when I embraced zero population growth and announced that, for the good of the planet, I wouldn't be having children. Maybe there are one or two other things I'm not remembering right now but that about covers it. So what's your point?

In *13th Gen*,[2] Neil Howe and Bill Strauss compare modern kids to other *bad* generations in America. Each was despised by the next-elder generation for being lazy, wild, uneducated, and

[1] Robert Townsend, *The B^2 Chronicles: How Not to Butt Heads with the Next Generation* (San Diego: Pfeiffer & Company, 1994), p. ix.
[2] Neil Howe and Bill Strauss, *13th Gen: Abort, Retry, Ignore, Fail?* (New York: Vintage, 1993), pp. 206-214. (The name refers to the 13th generation, starting from Benjamin Franklin's, to be Americans complete with federal government, flag and constitution.)

unredeemable. But in middle age and beyond, each of these bad generations distinguished itself for giving better than it got.

- The Cavalier Generation, born from 1615 to 1647 endured rebellions, wars, plagues, and outrageous taxes. They were noted for giving their children things their own parents had been unable to provide.
- The Liberty Generation, born from 1724 to 1741 produced most of the signatories for the Declaration of Independence and fought the war for independence from the Motherland. Years later they were prudent national leaders, intent on securing the peace for their children's children.
- The Gilded Generation, born from 1822 to 1842 was decimated by the American Civil War. In maturity they were hard-headed realists who led the nation through unprecedented technological and economic growth—not to mention America's version of the Victorian era.
- The Lost Generation, born from 1883 to 1900, grandparents to the Baby Boom, barely survived the war in Europe, then hit mid-life as the U.S. economy crashed in 1929. Former flappers and jazzmen became radical conservatives, thrifty protectors of community and family.

What about the new generation of Americans? What they become will have everything to do with what they experience. Much of that experience is out of their control—and ours. In some matters we'll just have to wait and see.

What we don't have to wait to see is that, in most ways, our children are remarkably like us. And, like us, they have to vote for themselves.

The real question for us Baby Boomers is, *What about our generation*? What are we becoming? What is our contribution, on a personal level, to what our children become when they're our age? Because that's the point. Human beings tend to grow into adults sooner or later, by hook or by crook. That's the testimony of time. Sure, there are a few missing civilizations—cultures that went away, absorbed by other cultures for better and worse. But not many. And none in a single generation. So, what kind of generation will *we* turn out to be before it's over? You do realize that it's not over.

So, if our kids are mostly normal, then …

Lighten up a little. Nurturing kids to maturity means celebrating *process, growth,* and *responsibility* even if it means giving up *control.*

Lemme be the first to admit it: Giving up control is hard. Remember the bell tower scene from Ron Howard's film *Parenthood?* A young man climbs into a bell tower with a high-powered rifle and starts shooting at people. It's all noise and bedlam. All of a sudden, through the chaos, someone points at a middle-aged man and shouts, "Hey! That's his father!"

Nobody wants that. So we develop the slightest imaginable tendency toward over-controlling our children, especially the older ones. And a lot of them grow up just the least bit tentative about making big life decisions like, *What should I wear?*

But really, that's probably not as serious as people say, and the children probably don't really grow up filled with resentment. Those stories are probably made up by children to scare us. They would most likely grow up to require years of therapy anyway, even if we didn't try to control every aspect of their lives. So, look, he'll carry on about this for a couple of more paragraphs because he's paid by the word. But, believe me, it's nothing new. You can just skip on down.

While we're on the subject of control, let's reconsider the notion of adolescent rebellion. Rebellion is a *very* strong word. Peasants and slaves rebel when they have nothing to lose; when losing everything—even dying in the streets—is less threatening than living another day with things as they are. People don't rebel against inconvenience or disagreement. People rebel against what they can no longer tolerate. Do the children in your life feel so oppressed they'd really rather die than keep living that way? If so, maybe you should be their liberator. If not, maybe we could tone down the language. Call it exploring the boundaries. Call it differentiating or role-taking. You can even call it acting out. But, unless they're storming the castle and setting fire to the crops, are you sure you want to call it rebellion?

Somebody said something about nobody learning from history. Here's one thing we learn from history: Human societies pull themselves together more often than they fall apart. I'm not saying our culture can't collapse, I'm just saying I think we have an obligation to look critically at the generation we can actually do something about before we hammer the one behind us. My question is: Seeing what we have to contend with now, and guessing at what's ahead, what sort of person do I need to be, and where will I get the resources to be such a person? If enough Baby Boomers answer that question so as to end our lives generously and well, I suspect the kids will be okay.

I know this opinion doesn't reflect the possibility of cataclysmic events. What if the world economy collapses? What if there's a really big war in Africa or Asia or Eastern Europe? What if there's a viral outbreak? What if a meteor grazes the earth and takes out half of humankind? If such things happen, God help us. If they don't, God help us anyway. We need all the help we can get to just be ordinary, decent, human beings.

Habilitate. He wouldn't know it, but about a decade ago, H. Stephen Glenn became one of my long-distance mentors. In his newsletter, *Sunrays*, Glenn described a conversation with his daughter on the subject of rehabilitation. She looked up the word and found it meant "to restore to former excellence." When he began to laugh, she asked what was so funny.

These days, the time it takes for kids to mature seems inflated. Humans, unlike dogs or mayflies, mature slowly anyway. For our kind it's not a couple of days or a couple of years. It's a couple of decades. Most of us don't really think most eighteen-year-olds are ready to be let loose on the world. It's not unusual for parents to support their offspring for another six, eight, even ten years into legal adulthood. Thirty percent of Americans in their twenties live with their parents.[3] Why? I think it's because they're *unhabilitated*.

"I was just thinking about all the people I work with. It is hard for me to believe that every struggling adolescent was once an excellent individual who forgot how. It is hard for me to believe that every struggling alcoholic was once an excellent recovering alcoholic and gave it up for some unknown reason. I can't believe that every chronically inadequate family was once an excellent family and lost sight of it. I can't believe that every struggling organization was once excellent at creating a nurturing atmosphere for employees and then decided to be discouraging instead. It is my impression that virtually all of the people I have served in my career have been struggling to attain something for the first time that had never been within reach for them."

Seeing my confusion, she tried to help by saying, "Daddy, if these people have not already achieved excellence, aren't you trying to redo something that was never done in the first place?"

As lights went off in my head I said, "Why didn't I think of that during all my years of higher education . . . Where were you about thirty billion dollars worth of federal programs ago with that kind of logic and insight?"

— **H. STEPHEN GLENN**[4]

The question is, whose responsibility would that be?

Am I missing something? Is the way we've been doing this working so well we just can't get enough? Is this so much fun that we couldn't dream of trying it another way? A shocking picture just presented itself to my sick mind. It's the image of a twenty-four-year-old woman, nursing at her mother's forty-six-year-old breast because the young woman is hungry and because she is, as yet, unweaned.

Please. Habilitate. Really.

[3] *Time*, June 9, 1997, pp. 67-68.
[4] *Sunrays*, December 1993, Sunrise Associates, 9700-C Fair Oaks Blvd., Fair Oaks, CA, 95628.

Habilitation takes time. This falls under the rubric of the sign on the wall in my Uncle Willard's boat shop:

> *How come there's never enough time to do the job right but there's always enough time to do it again?*

Well . . . I don't know. I wish I did, but I don't. I do believe with all my heart that this is too important to do poorly. Maybe because it seems like such a long-range project, like painting the Sistine Chapel. I know I've seen a lot of my friends get a little panicky when they realized their child would be graduating in a year—"God help us! *Not* a year! Two *semesters*! Nine months! He's totally unprepared! He can't clean his room properly, how can we trust him with, with . . . LIFE! Okay. Calm down. We have nine months. We can do this. We'll just have to crack down. We had him in nine months, we can finish him in nine months. Can't we?!"

No, Michelangelo, you can't.

It takes time to do it right. You can create a thoughtful inventory of what you think is missing. You can accept responsibility for the items you waited on until the last minute. You can conscientiously begin to fit (and retrofit) your child's knowledge, experience, and skillset. What you can't do is cram like you forgot there was a test tomorrow. It won't happen. And if you're thinking about making your daughter join the Army, forget about it.

If you find yourself in this situation—too much to cover, too little time—first, take a deep breath. Then, do the inventory. Accept responsibility. Develop a plan, first things first, knowing

some things can be learned after your kid is away at college, or on the job, or even in the Army.

This is what is known as *Plan B.* There's nothing wrong with Plan B. If you knew then what you know now, Plan A would have been better. But you didn't. So make Plan B as good as it can be.

Habilitation takes attention. If you've been waiting for my rant on Quality Time, here it is. Frank . . . ?

"I don't really have a lot of time for romance. In fact, I'm on deadline right now, so, as nice as a little foreplay would be, if we could cut to the chase, I promise you this will be a quality experience. Ooh, yeh, baby, baby."

I think that about covers it.

***Habilitation takes* flexibility, adaptability, negotiation** *in the context of clear values.* These are qualities of habilitated individuals. Once I know what my values are, about, say, dating or budget overruns, I have to live out those values with a sense of scale.

If my child constantly overspent her budget and always looked to me for a bailout, it would be unwise to rescue her this time. To do so would be to put off the painful lesson one more time, and probably make another deposit in my anger account (which is already overfunded from matters that have nothing to do with her). Since, however, she is normally thrifty but is a little overextended because she seized one opportunity too many, why not extend a line of credit and help her learn how to

FOR MORE ON DO-OVERS, GO TO PAGE 113.

use it? That seems to me like appropriate *flexibility*.

If my work situation changes and there's less disposable income for a time, why shouldn't everybody share in the belt-tightening? And if fortune swings the other way, why shouldn't we all benefit proportionally? That's *adaptability*.

If my child wants to negotiate a different curfew, a new division of household labor, an exception to the R-rated movie policy, why wouldn't I listen to her reasoning? I would. I did. In the process, she learned principles of full-disclosure and good-faith *negotiation*. We all won.

Which is what habilitation takes: On balance, everyone must win.

Habilitation takes shared trust. Ultimately, it comes down to trusting each other because the other is trustworthy. Untrustworthy parents raise cynical, bitter children. Untrustworthy children produce frowning, suspicious, over-sensitive parents. It's everyone for himself; nobody wins.

Trust is built one exchange after another for the life of the relationship. I don't think that means perfection. People mess up because, after all, we're people. We may be made, as I contend, in the image of God. But that image is tarnished by all the greasy things we do; it's slimed because we fail to do the obvious good. Maybe I should just speak for myself here; you may represent a much better class of citizen than me. But I doubt it. So, if perfection isn't attainable, how can we hope to trust?

I think trust is built on the agreement that we're in this together. That we're both doing it for the first time (even if you raised kids before, you never raised this one, and even if he had parents before, he never had you). I think trust is earned and maintained, not owed by either party.

What I think we do owe each other is do-overs. Trust, like every good thing we offer each other, is a taste of grace. I think trust is built on success and I also think trust rises from the ashes of failure when we own the failure and take an honest swing at doing it right the next time.

Do-overs are not so much for flagrant violations as for slips and foot-faults and falls. It's like a Mulligan in golf, offered because we're playing together, not against each other.

> What's the alternative to rebuilding broken trust? I mean, it's not like you can fire each other.

I have to be honest here: If your child is extraordinarily good, you may have to protect him from us. We're tough on exceptionally good people; always have been.

If your child is extraordinarily bad, you may have to protect us from him. There's a little Gary Gilmore in us all. If too much of it gets concentrated in one person we call him . . . Gary Gilmore. Or Charlie Manson. Or Jeffrey Dahmer. Or John Wayne Gacey . . .

Chances are, your child is neither extraordinarily good nor insidiously bad. Intelligence, strength, goodness—these attributes fall in a bell curve distribution: A few strong, a few weak, and the rest of us.

I think life usually makes sense. I've talked with kids who did very unusual things to hurt themselves or others and found, behind the outrageousness of it all, a thread of reason that was difficult to deny. I'm not saying a girl who cuts herself is sensible. I'm saying, given the strangeness of her life, cutting made sense at the time. Is it then okay for her to cut away? I don't think so. I don't think the scars think so or they would just disappear.

But I think I understand—as well as another person can—what was going on when she did it.

It's interesting how many people change destructive patterns and behaviors when they come to see them for what they are. I've seldom seen serious troubles reversed with the ease of turning off a light switch. But I've seen life-threatening patterns fade away when light came from the outside.

I've seen parents and children work out huge issues without intervention from doctors, lawyers, or tribal elders. Others have made peace with just a little assist, nothing really, no more than a referee.

So I say this, giving everyone the benefit of the doubt: If you've done everything you know to do; if you've stayed engaged with your kid through hard times and told your stories and explored the stories behind your child's stories; if you've asked for and received a little assist; if you've done all that and things are still weird, maybe it's time to entertain the likelihood that something is really, really wrong.

*If that appears to be the case, be realistic. Get help. You're not a failure; it's a bigger issue. If the house were burning, even if it were your mistake, you'd call the fire department—it's what they do.—**jb***

Begin where you are. Some of us care for young children and we can be proactive in fitting them with what it takes to become adults. Call it preventive maintenance and don't think for a second about what it costs.

The rest of us care for older children, even adult children. We'll be retrofitting our relationships. We have no choice but to be reactive in establishing these patterns. Had we known better, we would've done better. It's time to ask for do-overs and there's nothing wrong with that unless it

stems from malicious neglect. Even then—though it's a tougher sell—it's not impossible. It ain't over 'til it's over.

Sometimes I ask hurting parents, "If you knew then what you know now, would you have done it differently?"

They usually say, "Yeh, I'd have done it very differently." And sometimes they say what in particular they would undo if they could.

"Well *did* you know then what you know now?" I ask.

"No," they say, a little sadly.

"So, what you did made sense at the time? Given what you knew?"

"Yeh," they say. "For the most part."

"You know what?" I say, "I believe that. I just have one other question, okay?"

Still sad: "Yeh, okay."

"The question I have is, if you could get do-overs, what would you do *now*?"

That's the one question I have for you, too: What would you do if, starting today, you had do-overs with your kid?

What's the most significant thing you read or thought about in this chapter?

Why do you think that's so significant?

What do you think you might want to do about that?

Don't take my word for it. What did you read here that's worth checking with a kid?

All in One Boat

4.0

This much I know

for sure:

If raising adults

were easy, everyone

would do it.

The kids in Generation X are the children of the Me Decade. I'm not sure I like it, but I'm pretty sure it's true; I'm pretty sure it's a factor in how our children grow up.

How could it not be? Any more than our growing up years were, maybe not determined but certainly, *certainly* shaped by the men and women who raised us. Or did their best to raise us. In the end, that's as good as that ever got for as many generations as we can trace. And it's as good as it will get for as many more as we can imagine.

I don't always know what my best is. This much I know for sure: If raising adults were easy, everyone would do it.

We don't have to look far down the street to see everyone isn't doing it. The teacher in the class next door isn't raising adults. The neighbors across the street aren't. The manager at Burgerama can't seem to get his arms around it. Law enforcement doesn't have the picture. Music teachers and coaches? Sorry.

What's a mother to do?

Sometimes—forgive me, Mom—I think my parents missed raising an adult by as wide a margin as anyone I know. But not for lack of trying.

My dad is dead now and I believe I can speak frankly. He was a sweet man, a dear man, a caring, talented, charismatic man. He was an attractive, sexually compulsive, predatory man who did things that should have gotten him fired from a long series of ministerial jobs. He was an orphan, raised to breeding age by loving, generous siblings who did the best they knew how. Everything my father knew about being a dad was picked up from amateurs or made up as he went along. But, come to think of it, that's the way it happens for most of us. How many dads do you know who had a really well-formed role model for parenting? A few I hope; I bet not many.

My role model wrestled with deep shadows that pinned him most of the time. He blew a twenty-three-year marriage to my mom by serial adulteries, most of which she never knew about. A second marriage lasted about as long as the first, then unravelled because he was such a sanctimonious sinner. Who wants to be constantly judged by someone whose behavior belies his holier-than-God attitude? So my father's second wife said goodbye. And he was alone.

I know these things because, when I was thirty-seven years old and wrestling my own shadows, my father came clean with me. I was back in the ol' hometown for my twentieth high school reunion—an entirely different story and weird in its own right. Being with my dad on this occasion was surreal. We drove around town and he pointed out the places he met women—romantic spots like the airport parking lot. There was no bragging, only confession, which made hating him very difficult. I wanted to. He told me he was never faithful to my mother and I wanted to hate him.

But I couldn't; he wasn't that guy anymore. He was broken, useless, empty-handed, brought full circle to live again among his loving, generous siblings who cared so much for him it didn't matter that, at the end, he had nothing anyone really needed. He just *was*.

I sat across from him in a little cafe near the Gulf of Mexico, near the mouth of the Ochlockonee River. I could hardly believe most of what he was saying, except I couldn't help believing it. I knew he was unfaithful to my mom; I had a half-brother to prove it. But *never* faithful? Of course it was true. It explained so much.

What I *really* couldn't believe was how much like him I had become.

My compulsions are different from my father's. He acted *out*, so of course he got caught. The wonder is how long he got away with it. I act *in*. Had I been stronger, I might've gotten away with it forever. These are only details. I'd like to be judgmental. I'd like to say I'm a better man than my father. The problem is, I've failed in every way I've been seriously tempted. I haven't done what he did, but I haven't been seriously tempted to do what he did. I'd like to think, if I were tempted to act out like my father, God would rescue me from the serious wrongs he did. My dad would've liked to think the same thing. We both would wish it were that simple.

In the end I couldn't hate my father because, at long last, he *was* my father. No better, no worse, no different.

I remember thinking, if this guy, who for fifty years preached about God's love, expressed to humankind in Jesus . . . if this man, this preacher, finally came to *believe* that good news because he had nothing left—no props, no reputation, no work to do . . . if God can reach *this* guy, I thought, then God can reach anyone. God can reach me.

I don't know how my mother's parents started; they ended up just bewildered. All the years I knew him, my grandfather was a sweet, passive man who spent a lot of time on the porch, smoking Prince Albert in a can. My grandmother was as angry as anyone I ever knew. She lost heart and died in her sixties, while I was quite young. They were a combined family: the widow and the traveling salesman; her children and theirs. He stopped traveling to cultivate the land she inherited from her first husband, then lost the farm. They took what was left and moved to the city where, I suppose, they lost themselves. He was chronically underemployed, she had her hands full raising a bunch of children. He grew more detached, her anger deepened. I don't think they were bad. Just lost in America.

My mom was the youngest. She went straight from high school to work and married a sailor who didn't go overseas but was distant and secretive anyway. She put him through college, then graduate school. As far back as that, she had an inkling he might not be quite as good as he appeared. But she didn't believe it. He was a ministerial student. They had a young daughter, then a son. She *wouldn't* believe it.

Every day of her adult life, my mom did everything she could to pay the mortgage and keep the lights on. Not that we were poor—just working class, living paycheck to paycheck, always in debt, our upward mobility almost imperceptible, never any closer to financial stability. To say my mother's life was disappointing is no overstatement. Her emotions were rubbed raw, exposed to the air, painful to touch.

Then one day she couldn't refuse to believe things were as bad as things were. My father got the same young woman pregnant twice, in a year, and that was that. They forgot to pick me up from church the night my mom found out about the second pregnancy. I walked home in the dark, bitter and feeling sorry for myself. They stayed up all night, doing whatever it is people do on the last night of a long, unhappy marriage. At dawn, my mother came into my bedroom and watched me for awhile. She sat on the edge of my bed. She put her head on my chest and cried. I pretended to be asleep. She cried for a year.

I don't know if anyone outside our household knew my mom had a sharp edge. I don't think so. She hid it in a sheath of Southern congeniality. That's often the way of that world; nice seems more important than good, or true, or authentic. Those are acknowledged virtues, but harder to come by. Nice can be summoned at will by the well bred and the strong. But niceness and congeniality wear thin under pressure, and my mother was always under pressure. So the blade was bared and we got cut from time to time—at least I did. Usually, I pretended to be asleep.

It may not matter. These days my mom has no edge at all. She seems mellow and grateful to be alive. Her memory is mushy after a brain tumor and surgery. And chemotherapy. And radiation.

A couple of years before the tumor, we started making real peace, my mom and me. By the time she got sick, I was no longer afraid to be with her. I don't think she was afraid to be with me either. I was no longer passive-aggressive with her and she didn't vent her anger at me. We went as far as we could in making amends. A wide gulf remained between our perceptions about a lot of things, but not between us. Mother's Day was no longer a crisis.

Two decades after it was too late to do it as a family, my dad and I and my mom and I learned to treat each other well in real life—which is to say, behind closed doors. We treated each other as well in secret as we appeared to treat each other in public in those idealized years before our nuclear family exploded in sexual craziness and anger and withdrawal.

We finally got it. It wasn't tidy but I believe it was real. Toward the end, no one needed permission to tell the truth. We each took responsibility for our actions and attitudes. We experienced and expressed a pretty complete range of emotions. Toward the end, we were *adult* with each other.

I marvel that it took so long. I marvel that it happened at all.

Try this on for size. It's called Hidden Meanings.

[*Living Room. A parent and kid are toe-to-toe. The kid speaks first to us.*]

Kid: I said,

[*Now the kid turns on the parent, fists clenched, screaming.*]
Get off my back!

[*The kid speaks right to us, earnest.*]

But what I really meant was, Please don't treat me like an idiot. Don't embarrass me anymore. Don't look at me like you're sorry I was born. We both know I was wrong—please don't rub it in.

I said, Get off my back. I *meant*, Could we please just do the last five minutes over again? Could we just, please, take it all back and do it again?

[*Kitchen. Parent and kid are agitated. The parent speaks first to us.*]

Parent: I said,

[*Now the parent pivots and slaps the top of the table, growling.*]

Why don't you just grow up!

[*The parent sits at the table, weary, and speaks right to us.*]

What I really meant was, You *are* growing up. You're growing up and it scares me.

I keep squeezing when I know I should lighten up. But . . . well, you're not perfect—and I'm afraid. I . . . I guess I'm afraid I've failed. I look at your bedroom and, deep down, I know it's not that big a deal—but I look in your room and I think I failed to teach you about responsibility. You forget to call when you're gonna be late and—I mean, I used to do the same thing! I'd get all involved in whatever I was doing and lose track of time. But when you do that, I worry that I've failed to teach you about caring.

I know that's stupid. But it's how I feel sometimes.

[*Living room. Kid has an exaggerated, "gimme a break" look. The kid speaks first to us.*]

Kid: I said,

[*Now the kid speaks sarcastically to the parent.*]

I was just kidding! Get over yourself! Man!

[*The kid addresses us again, kicking one toe into the carpet, looking uncomfortable, glancing up.*]

What I really meant was, I wish I hadn't said it, okay? It was stupid and untrue. I wasn't thinking.

I didn't mean to hurt you—not really—not when I saw it in your eyes. I wanted to die when I saw it in your eyes. You're, like, the adult. I'm not supposed to be able to get to you. I guess that's why I push sometimes. Just to see if I can sting you. Usually, I can't. And when I do—when I *did*—it felt really bad. *Really* bad.

I wish I could've said, I'm sorry. That's really hard for me . . .

[*Living Room, the parent speaks first to us.*]

Parent: I said

[*Now the parent turns on the kid gesturing, shouting.*]

As long as you live under my roof, you'll obey my rules!

[*The parent collapses onto the sofa and talks to us.*]

But I guess what I really meant is, well . . . I feel like we're falling apart—you know? I'm frustrated. It comes out as anger. I used to be your best friend. That's true, isn't it? Did I have that upside down too? Oh, God. I hope not.
I never wanted to squash you. I just wanna know you. I wanna be part of your life. I wish I could've said, *I'm afraid; please talk to me* . . .
That's really hard for me. I guess you know that.

[*Bedroom. The kid leans against the wall, exhausted.*]

Kid: I said,

[*The kid springs to action, slamming the door, shouting.*]

Fine! Perfect! I'm outta here!

[*The kid drops onto the bed and talks to us.*]

What I think I meant is . . . well, I *wanna* be close, you know? But not like before—not like I was still a kid. I *am* a kid—I know

that—but please don't treat me like a baby. It seems like the closer I get to freedom, the more you put the squeeze on me. I keep pulling away because I don't know what else to do. I wanna be close, but not like that . . . That—Just not like that, okay?

[*The kid is startled by a knock at the door. We follow the gaze to the closed door and hear the parent's voice from the other side.*]

Parent: Hey? (clearing throat) Can I come in?

[*The kid looks back at us, conflicted, uncertain. The lights fade to black.*] [1]

Raising adults isn't a bit easy. It's so hard I don't believe anyone can do it alone. I'm not just talking about the village it takes to raise a child. What I mean is, honestly, the job is so big and takes so long, it may have to be finished by the adult child.

The job may never be really finished. Seventy-five years may not be long enough to raise an adult. Not if I'm the adult. I'm pretty clear about this.

But if the goal is preparing people to keep growing until they're done or run out of days—whichever comes first—I think eighteen years or thereabouts is plenty.

Are there exceptions? Sure. They're exceptional.

But two decades is long enough to prepare most ordinary humans to finish the job. It's enough time to lead kids into the experiences they

[1] A slightly different version appeared in *EdgeTV*, edition 20. Edge Communications, Inc., Box 35005, Colorado Springs, CO 80935, 800-616-3343.

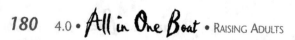

have to have, to help them gain the personal and relational skills they need to get on with their lives. It's long enough to furnish them with an emotional vocabulary they can expand and deepen along the way. In eighteen years or so, we can help kids see how able they are, how valuable, how effective they can be when they formulate plans and act on them, when they build alliances and honor them, when they make promises and keep them. Kids can learn to know themselves, learn what it takes to know others, to function in complex societies, deal with uncertainty and disappointment, to make wise choices and live with the outcomes, good and bad.

Every old man complains of the growing depravity of the world, of the petulance and insolence of the rising generation.

> —*Dr. Samuel Johnson, 1752*

It doesn't take a lifetime to cover that ground. It only takes a lifetime to master it—or find out we need help and grace to get where we hoped we were going.

True then, true today: Children and parents driving each other nuts for as long as anyone cared to keep records. What may be different at the intersection of *these* generations is, now we know what to do.

Seriously, we *know* what to do. We know the skillset our kids need to make it in the real world and we know, more or less, what it takes to learn those skills. We know, in a place deep inside us, what it takes to teach those skills.

The question is, Do we have the heart for it?

Do we have the heart to raise adults?

One of the many wakeup calls in my life as a father was the jarring realization that—because my daughter and I are both Christians—Kate is my sister as well as my daughter.

My daughter, my sister, my daughter, my sister, slap, slap, slap!
  Am I stuck in a Jack Nicholson movie or does this change things?

This changes everything. How can I be condescending, in the negative sense, to my daughter, my sister, Kate? And how can I fail to condescend in the positive sense, to kneel if that's what it takes to look in her eyes and try to understand as much as another can understand? She is not my property, not my pet, not my alter ego. She is a mirror in which I see myself because, for better and worse, she's just like me.

That realization hasn't done me a bit of harm. It's the truest thing about Kate and me. Sure I'm farther up the road, but it's the same road.

Just like Kate, I'm doing life for the first time and I'm not a hundred percent sure I get it. I don't think Kate, nor anyone in her generation really, is shocked by that. I don't think they ever bought the pretense to begin with—one of the reasons I have great hope for them. They know we're in this together, whether we know it or not.

Well, I know. I figured it out a little bit at a time until I stopped pretending to be the great white father. Feel free to replace that characterization with whatever suits your gender and ethnicity.

Once I stopped pretending—and it's fair to say I was sputtering out of gas as the bus coasted to a stop—I started figuring out what to do. It was so simple, I don't know how I could've missed it.

You ready?

I started acting like a human being. I began to acknowledge the most obvious thing about me, which is I'm just another guy. No better, no worse, no different from you. Or Kate. Which, of course, means I had to start treating Kate like a human being.

How could anything this obvious be so difficult?

For me, it's difficult because I'm self-centered, self-righteous, and self-absorbed. I imagine the sun and moon revolve around me. The tide rises to greet me and withdraws depressed when I leave. I expect every driver to watch out for me, every clerk to hustle for me, every clock to tick to the rhythm of my precious heartbeat.

I'm such an ass. I'm embarrassed by this, but I'd be less than honest if I didn't admit it. This may not be your problem. You may be a better woman than me. I hope so.

It is my problem and I've come to the conclusion that, if I were going to get much better, I would have by now.

I'm not.

What I am doing is—dare I steal one more time from A.A.?—I'm learning to *surrender my life and my will to God* on something that's beginning to look vaguely like a daily basis.

I'm learning to put first things first.

I'm learning to seek to understand first, then to be understood.

I'm learning to value serenity instead of passivity; courage instead of brashness; wisdom instead of wishful thinking.

I'm learning, growing, finishing the job my parents began; finishing the work of becoming an adult.

This is hard, honest work. I need all the help I can get from Susan and Kate, from my ailing mother, from my extended family and my friends. I need help from my Creator and if, as some think, there is no Creator, then I really need help.

I'm getting help from these sources and quite a few more in the village that's still raising me.

Don't kid yourself—I'm a man with all the rights and responsibilities that come with being an adult. Don't let *me* kid you—I'm not done yet.

🏃 What's the most significant thing you read or thought about in this chapter?

🏃 Why do you think that's so significant?

🏃 What do you think you might want to do about that?

🏃 Don't take my word for it. What did you read here that's worth checking with a kid?

Acknowledgments

I'm grateful for the kindness of my family and friends.

- **Alice Shi**, **Ben Behimer**, **Brian Boyle,** and **Eli Jaeger** offered their thoughts and feelings generously. Ben allowed me to include his remarkable poem (page **106**). They are good friends, each of them—lifelong friends, I expect. I'm really glad about that.
- **The Hoovers** of Piney Ridge fed me body and soul while I wrote. And they made me laugh! And they gave me Susan!
- My good neighbors at **Einstein Bros.** provided Diet Coke, warm asiago cheese and cranberry bagels and never once showed me the door.
- **H. Stephen Glenn** and **Jane Nelson** broke new ground for me in the '80s with *Developing Capable People.*
- The folks at **Piñon Press** are taking a chance on this book. I'm happy they're willing. I hope they guessed right. Special thanks to **Ray Moore** (for designing the book, then designing it again), **Brad Lewis**, **Terry Behimer**, the courageous **Sue Geiman**, and **Toben Heim** (my Champion and friend).
- The extraordinary people of North County, San Diego—especially Bob and Suzie Rantzow, the **Solana Beach Presbyterian Church** and **San Dieguito High School District**—trusted me to work all this out. I'll never forget them.
- My mom, **Mary Ruth Jackson**, is a heroine. She faced the Fear every day, doing the work of two people. My dad, **Millard Hancock**, failed as often as he succeeded. But he finished well, trusting Jesus to do what only Jesus can do. I hope to end as well.
- **Kate Hancock** allowed me to tell my story—which includes parts of hers— without once asking me to pretend things are better or worse or different than they are. She is a magnificent woman.
- **Susan Hancock** was my best friend before I knew it. She is still, through fortune's outrageous slings and arrows. I never dreamt it could be this good. I want it to never end.

GET TO *REALLY* KNOW SOMEONE.

What's Your Story?

This interactive guide is designed to help people tell their stories and develop deeper relationships by recounting their experiences, feelings, values, and beliefs with others. Start talking about —and listening to—the things that really matter.

What's Your Story?
(Toben and Joanne Heim) $10